CREATIVE CANVAS

WORLD OF COLORING FOR EVERYONE

Kami Moon

The Creative Canvas

In a land where imagination knew no bounds and colors held the power to shape reality, there existed a magical city known as Chakatra. Within this mystical world, every hue and shade were alive, alive with energy and waiting to be woven into stories. And at the heart of Chakatra, there lay a remarkable coloring book that held the key to unlocking the magic within.

Legend spoke of "The Creative Canvas," a coloring book unlike any other. It was said to have been crafted by a long-lost artist, whose dreams were infused into each page, giving life to a multitude of captivating realms. Those who ventured into its pages embarked on a journey beyond the ordinary, where creativity knew no bounds and the extraordinary was merely a stroke of a color away.

The first page of "The Creative Canvas" held a gateway to Chakatra itself. As you colored the swirling portal, a sense of anticipation filled the air. With the final flourish of your chosen color, the portal would spring to life, transporting you into a world of your own creation. Each page thereafter was a new land to explore, from the whispering Forest, where trees hummed tunes of ancient melodies, to the dazzling Stars, where they sparkled like constellations.

But it wasn't just the places that came alive; the characters leaped from the pages as well. The mischievous foxes of Vivid Vale would scamper about, waiting for your artistic hand to guide their antics. The valiant knights would stand tall, ready for epic quests painted by your imagination. Every stroke of color breathed life into these beings, granting them stories and personalities, each more enchanting than the last.

As you journeyed deeper into the book, you would find yourself in the heart of the Realm, a realm of pure creativity. Here, the rules of reality were mere suggestions, and the colors you wielded had the power to shape the very fabric of existence. With every brushstroke, you could bend rivers, conjure storms, and create sunsets that painted the skies with a thousand shades of wonder.

"The Creative Canvas" was not just a coloring book; it was an invitation to rediscover the magic within yourself. It beckoned you to embrace the artist within, to explore the limitless boundaries of your imagination, and to experience a world where colors danced, dreams thrived, and stories became your reality.

With every page turned and every color chosen, you would find yourself not only coloring the book but also coloring your own world with the vibrancy and brilliance of Chroma. So, embark on this coloring adventure, unleash your creativity, and let "The Creative Canvas" guide you through a realm where dreams and colors intertwine, waiting for your touch to awaken the magic. Get ready to paint your own story in the most wondrous hues, for within these pages, the extraordinary becomes your masterpiece.

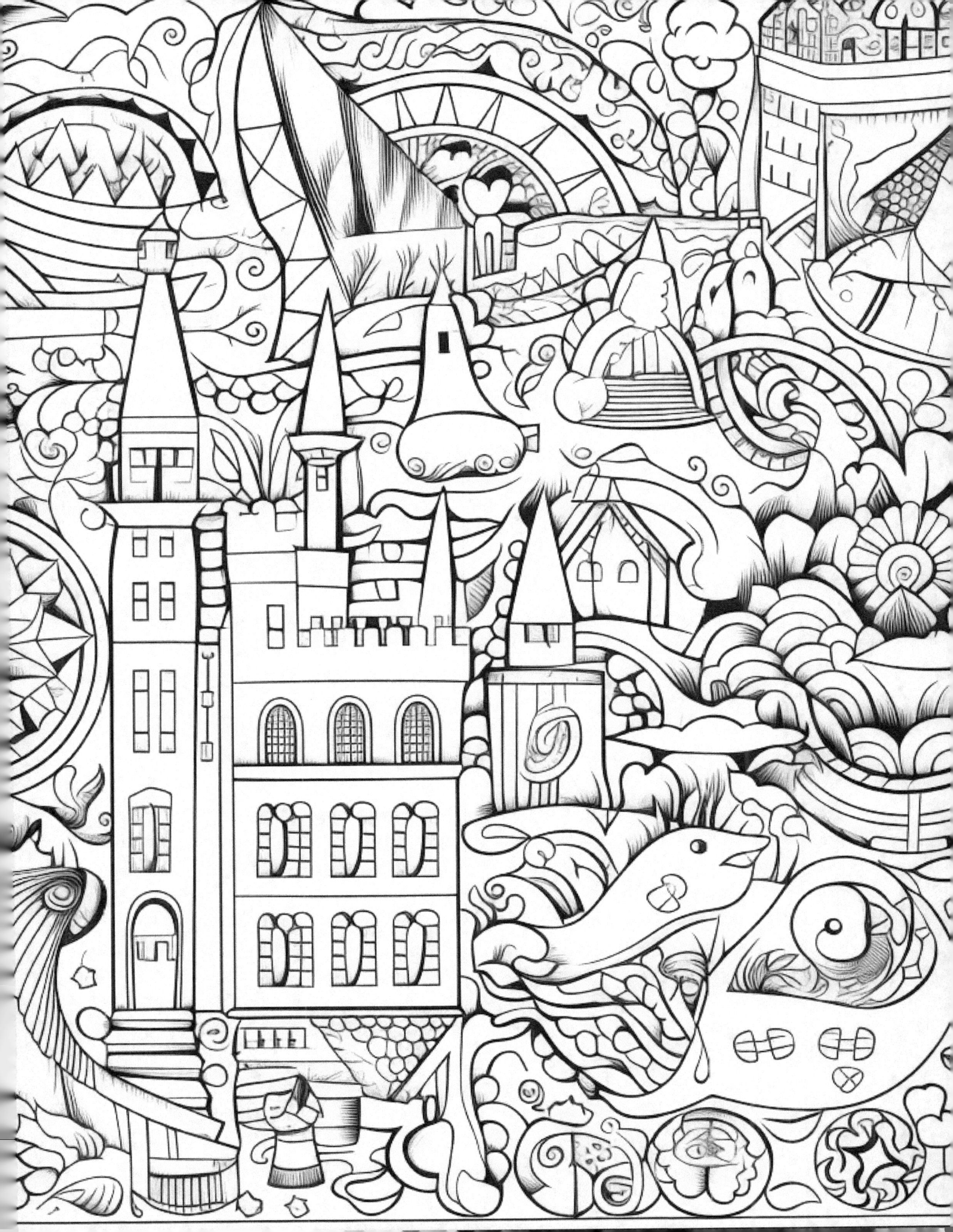

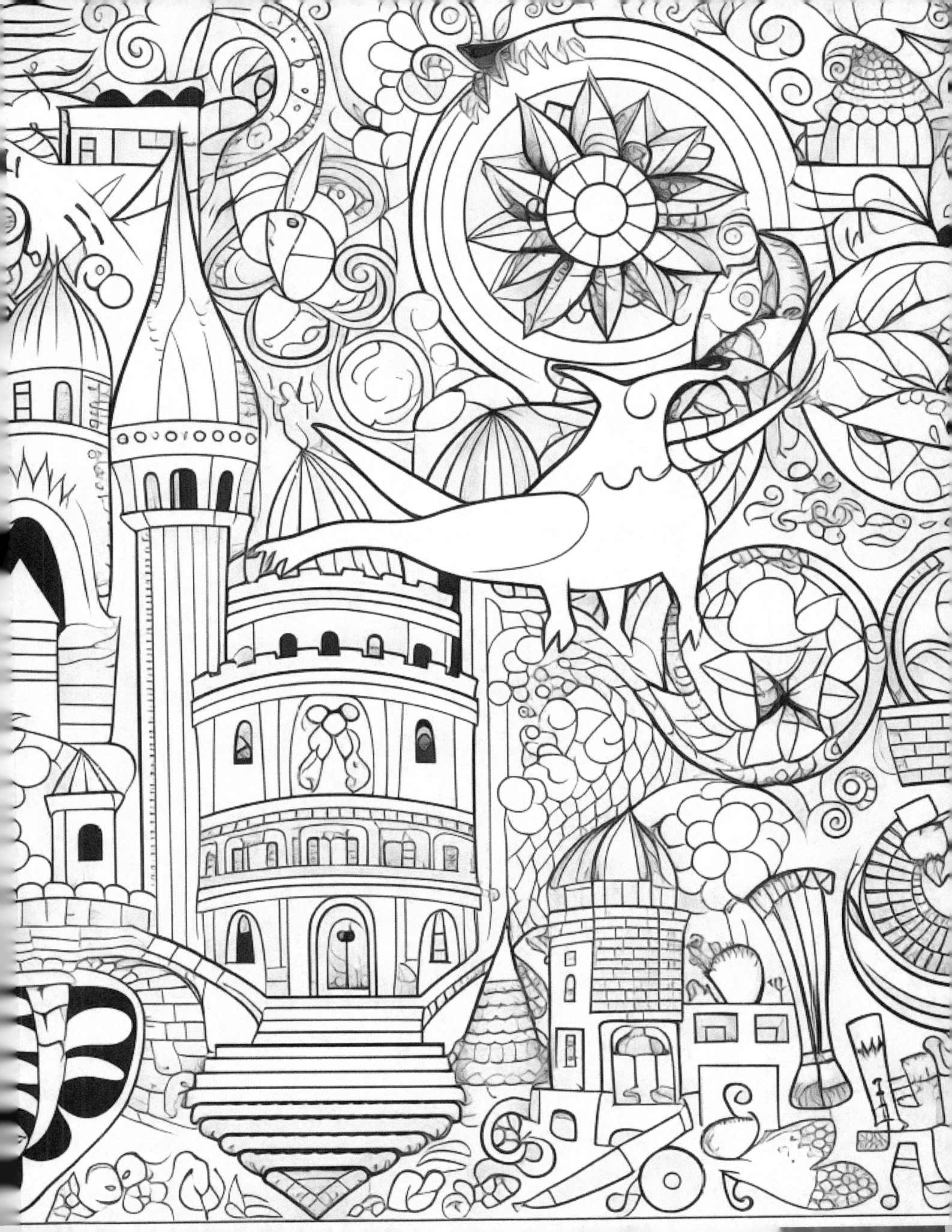

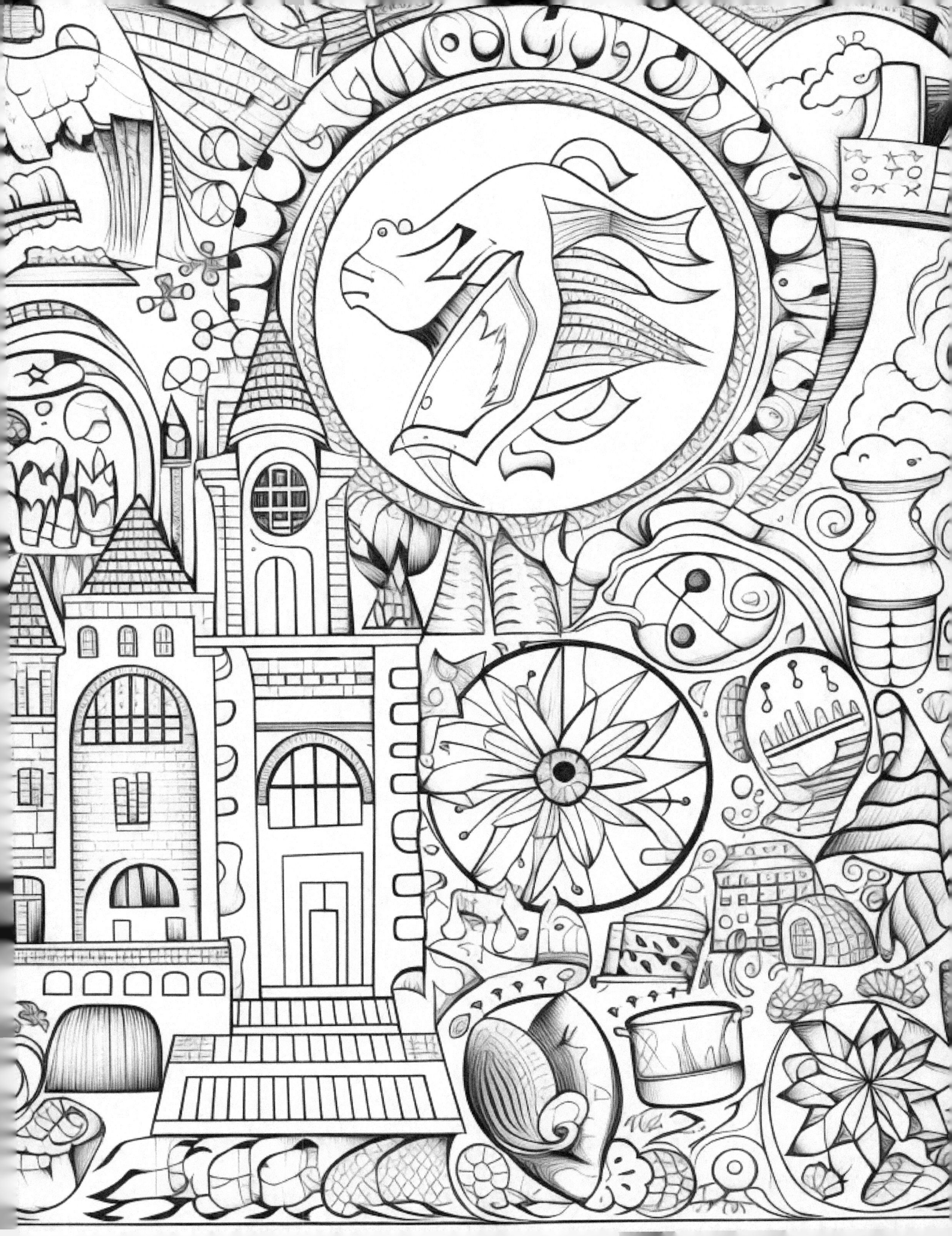

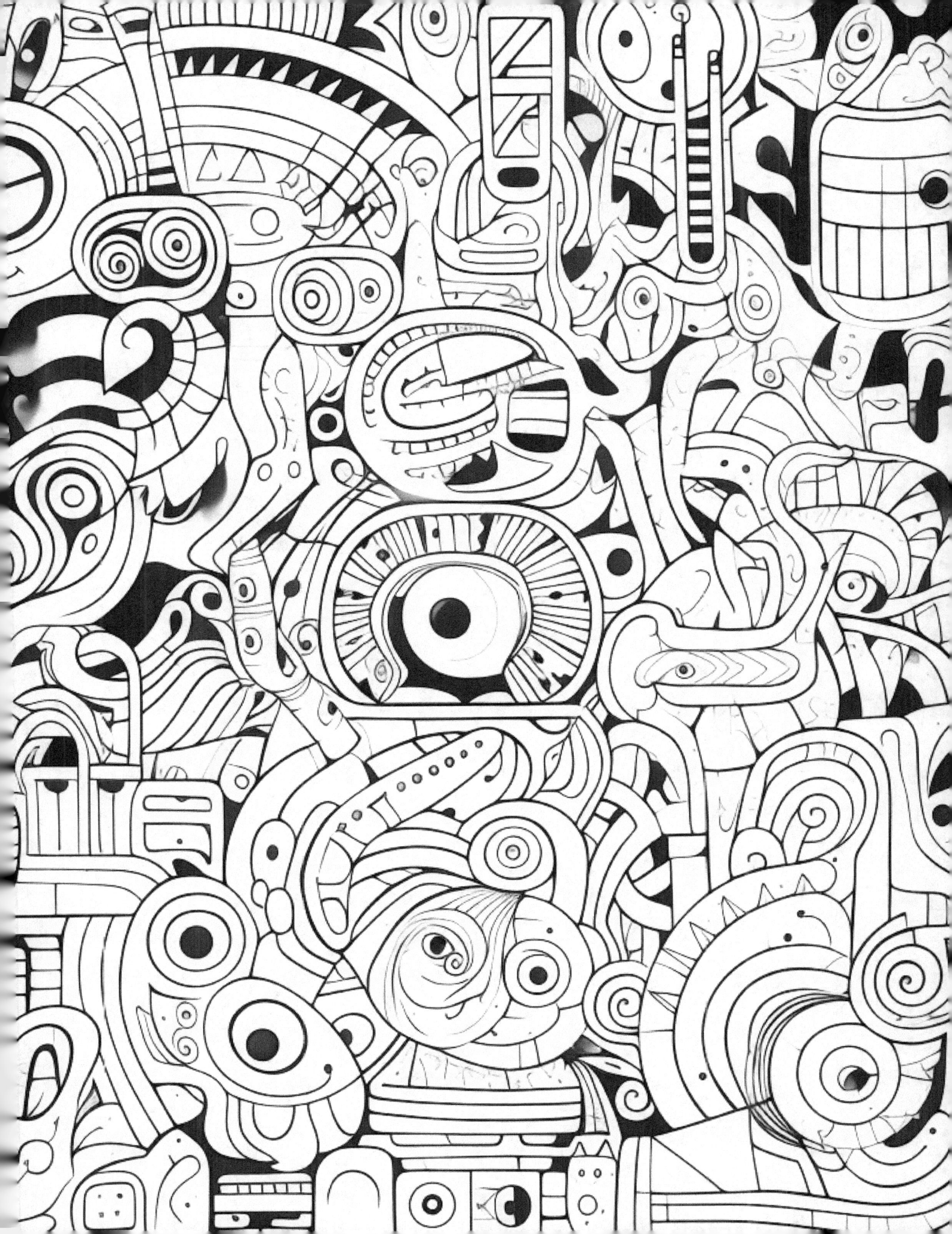

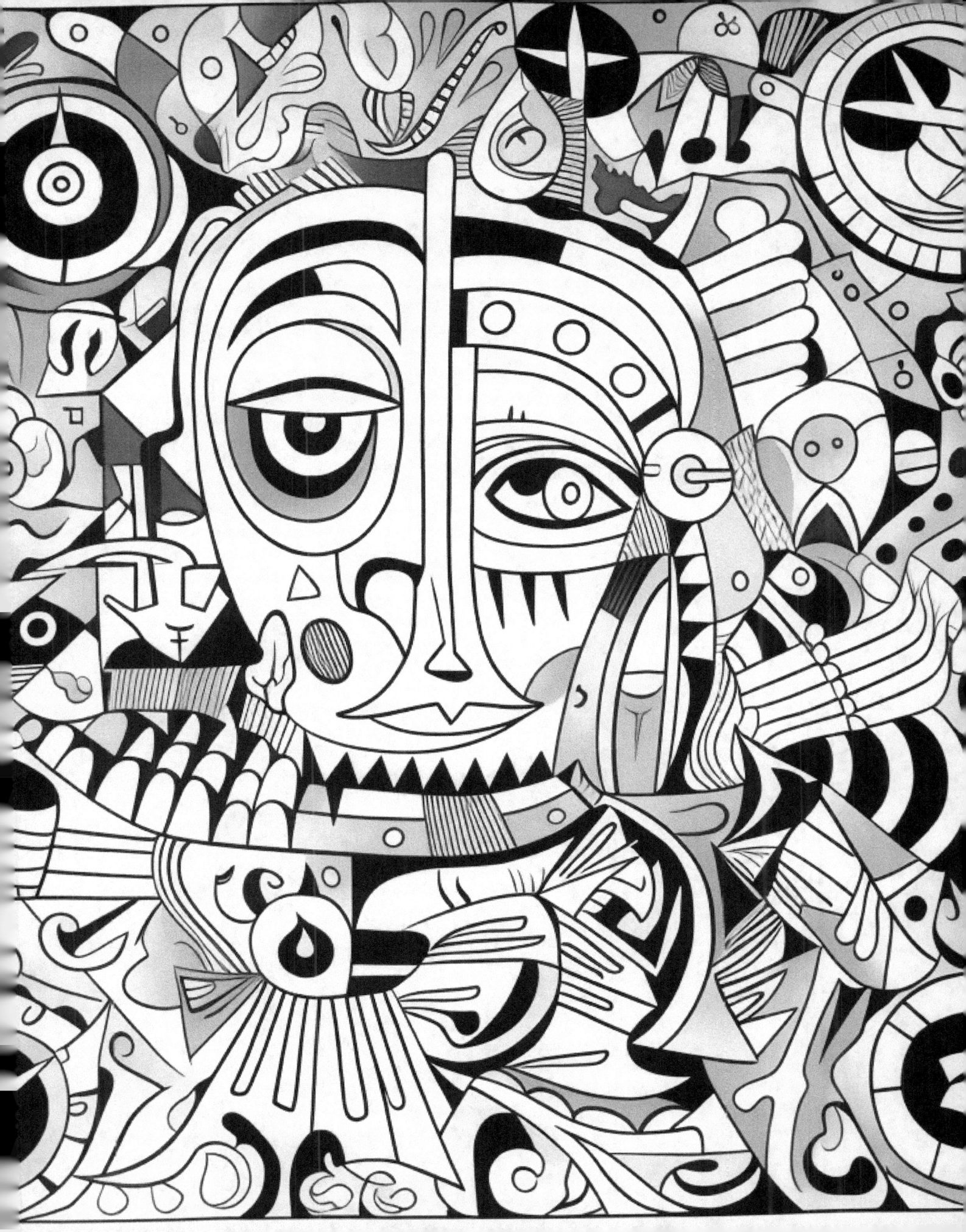

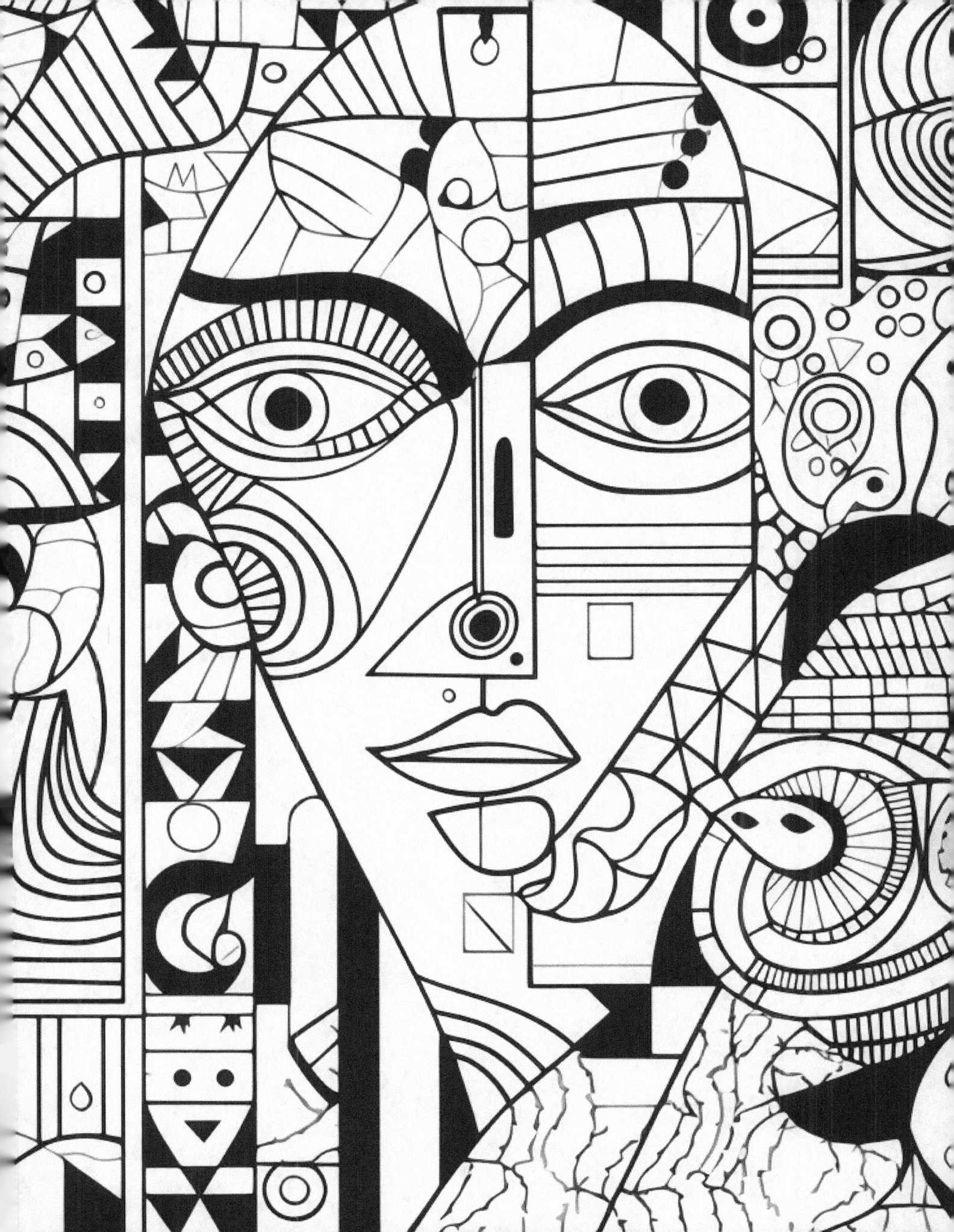

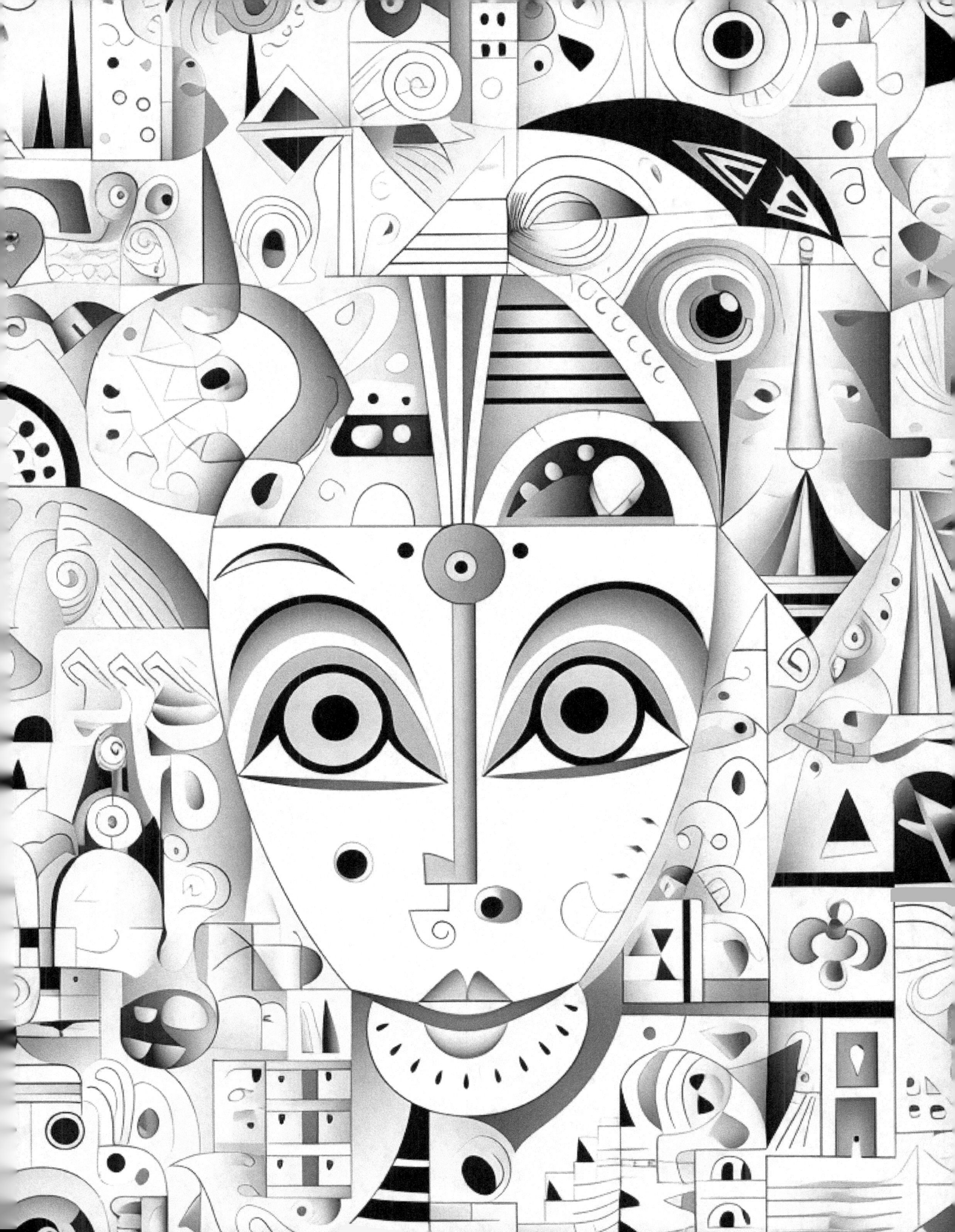

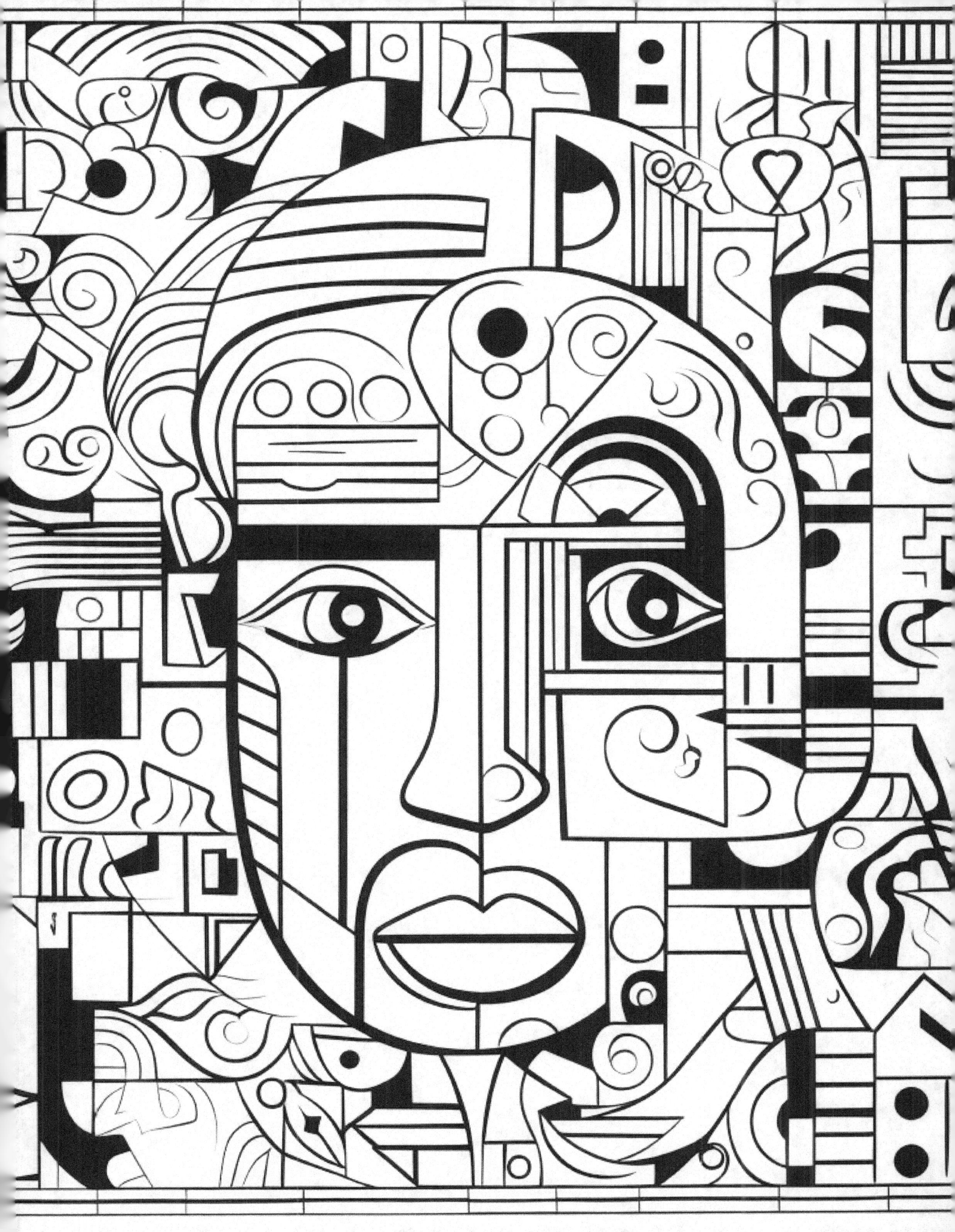

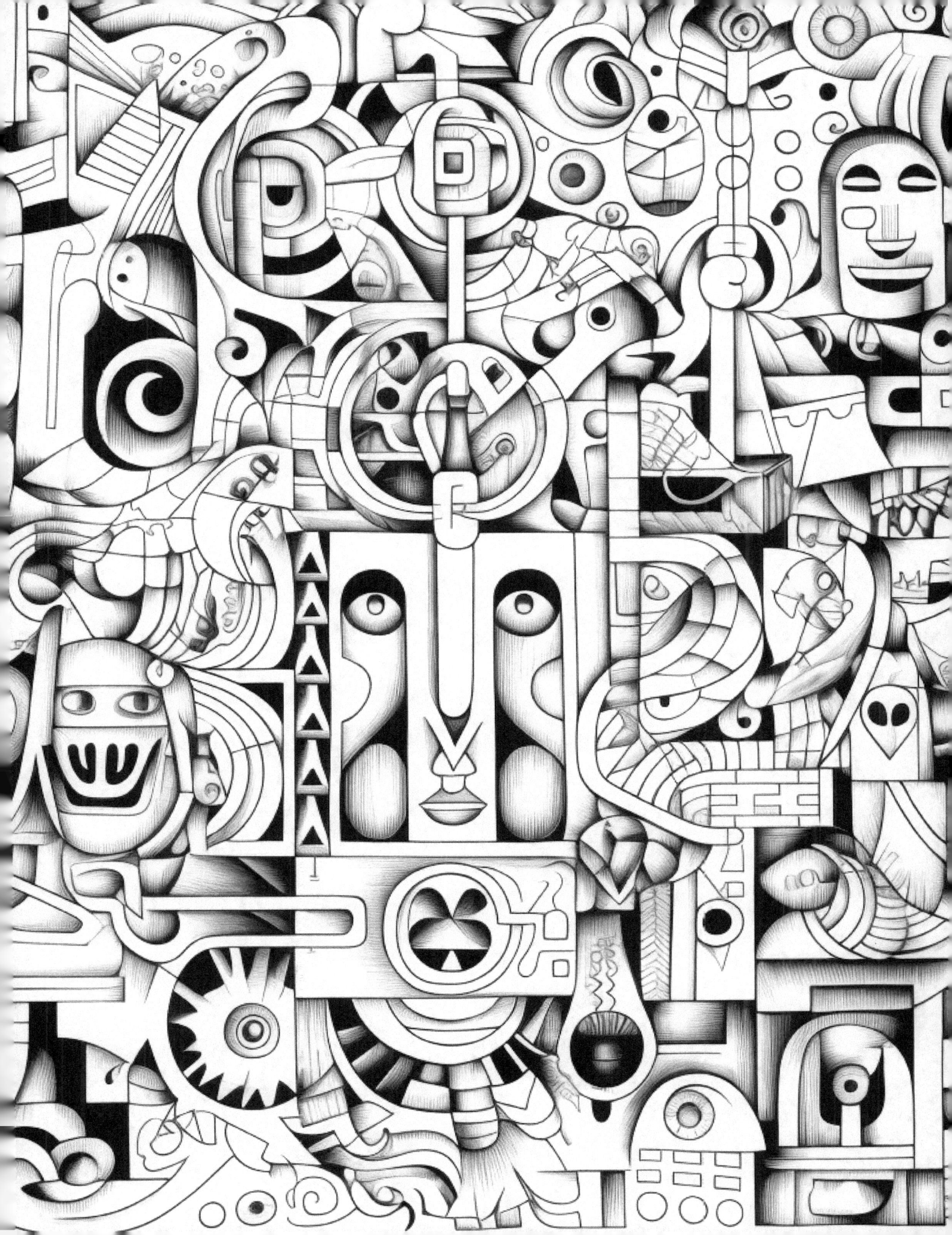

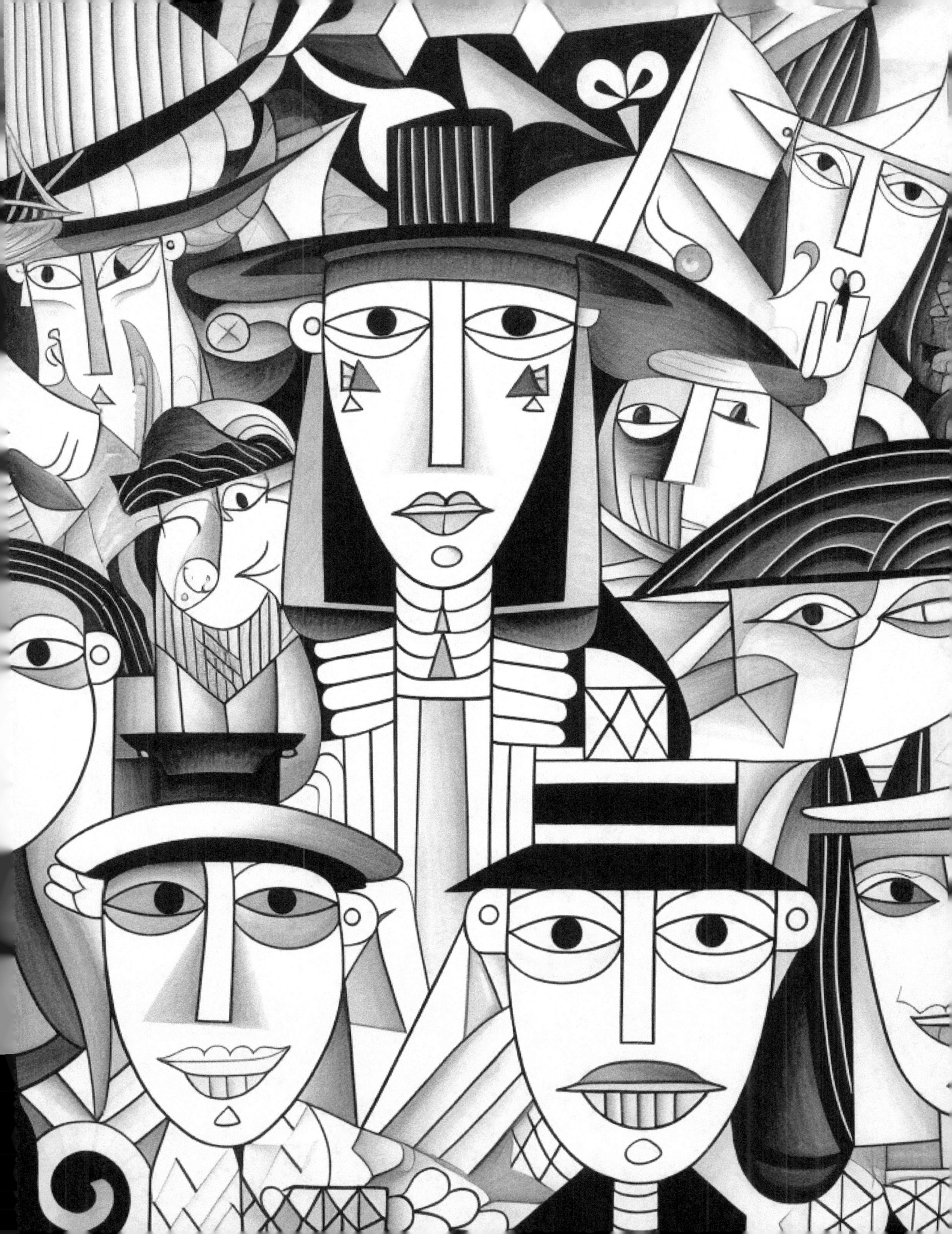

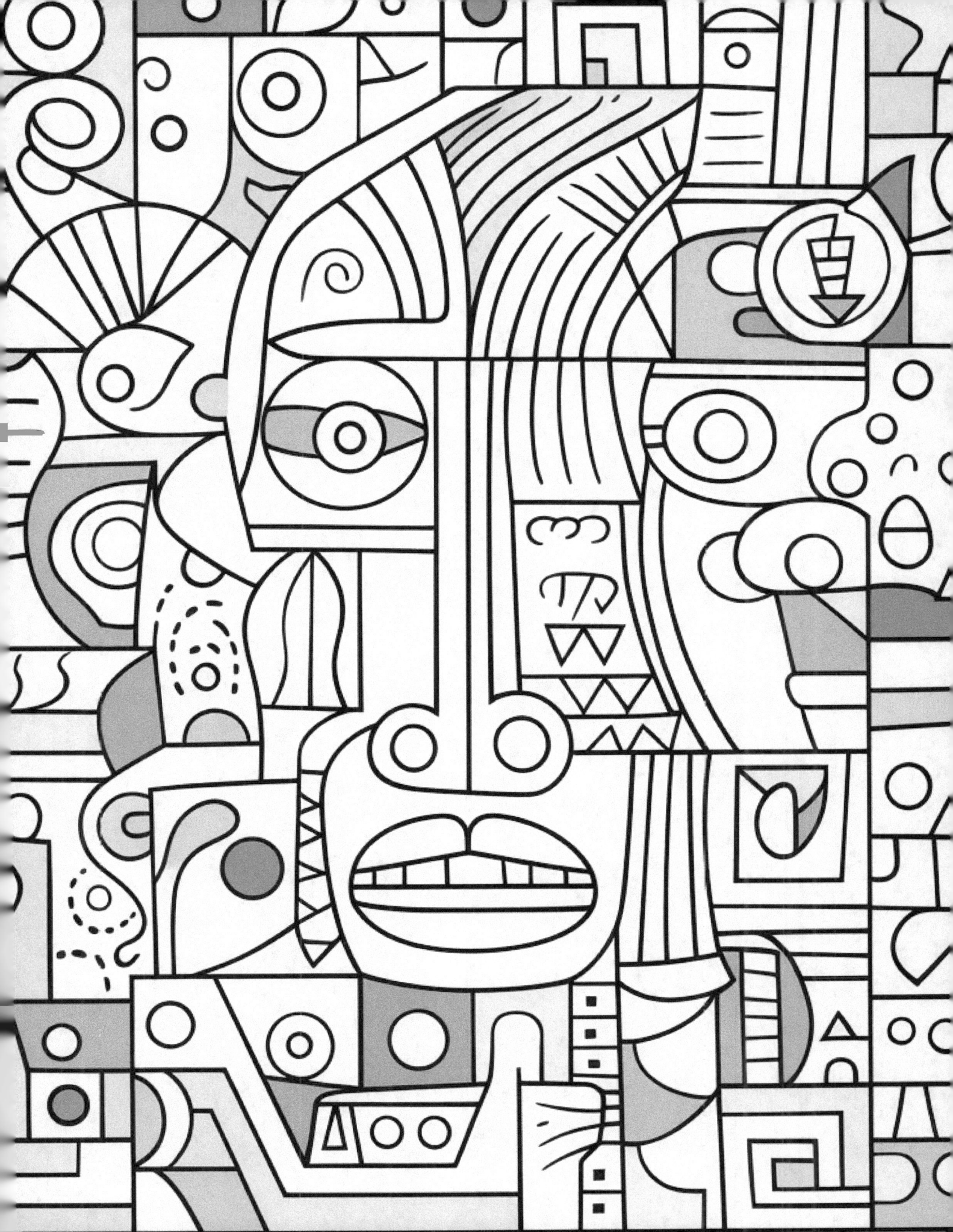

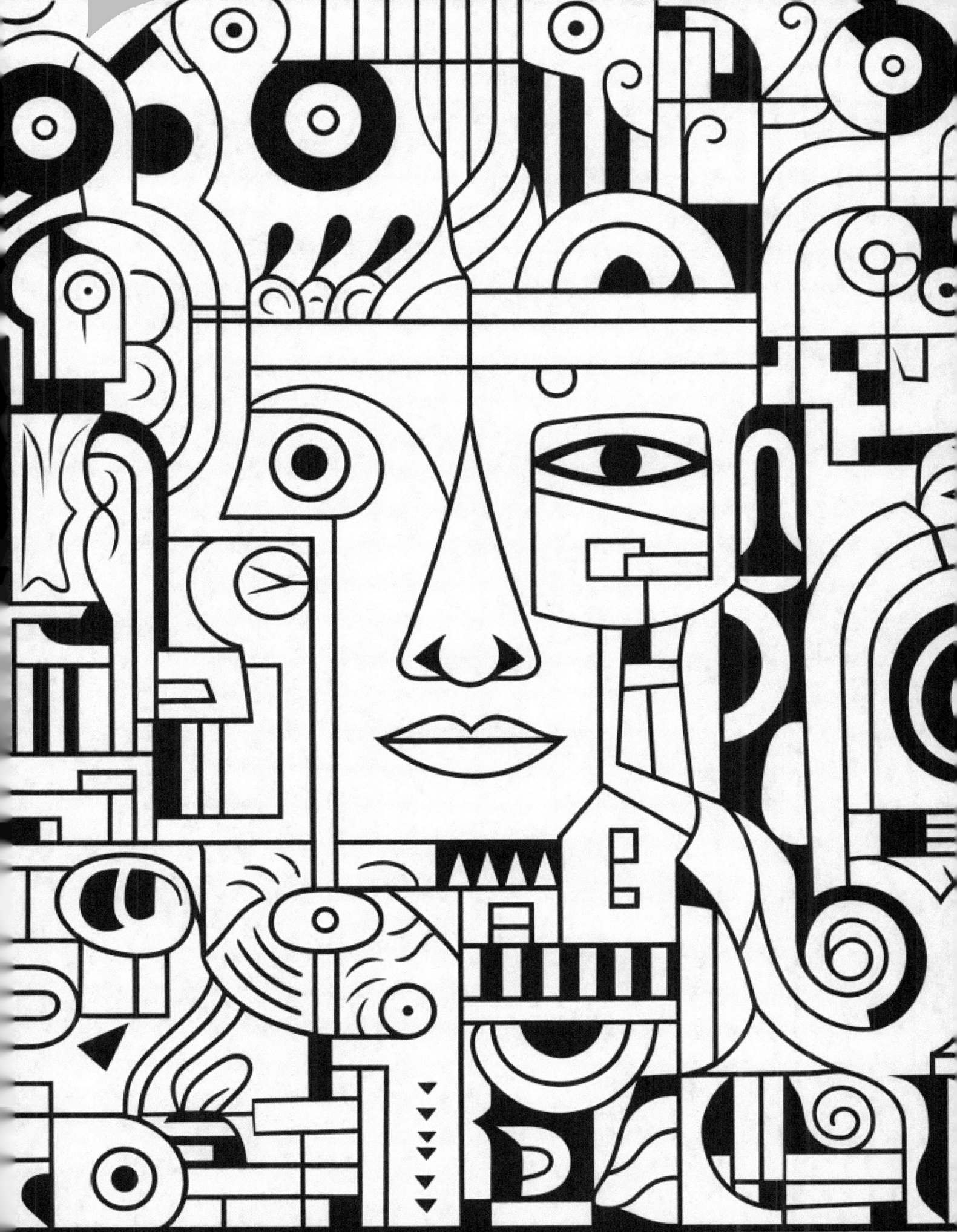

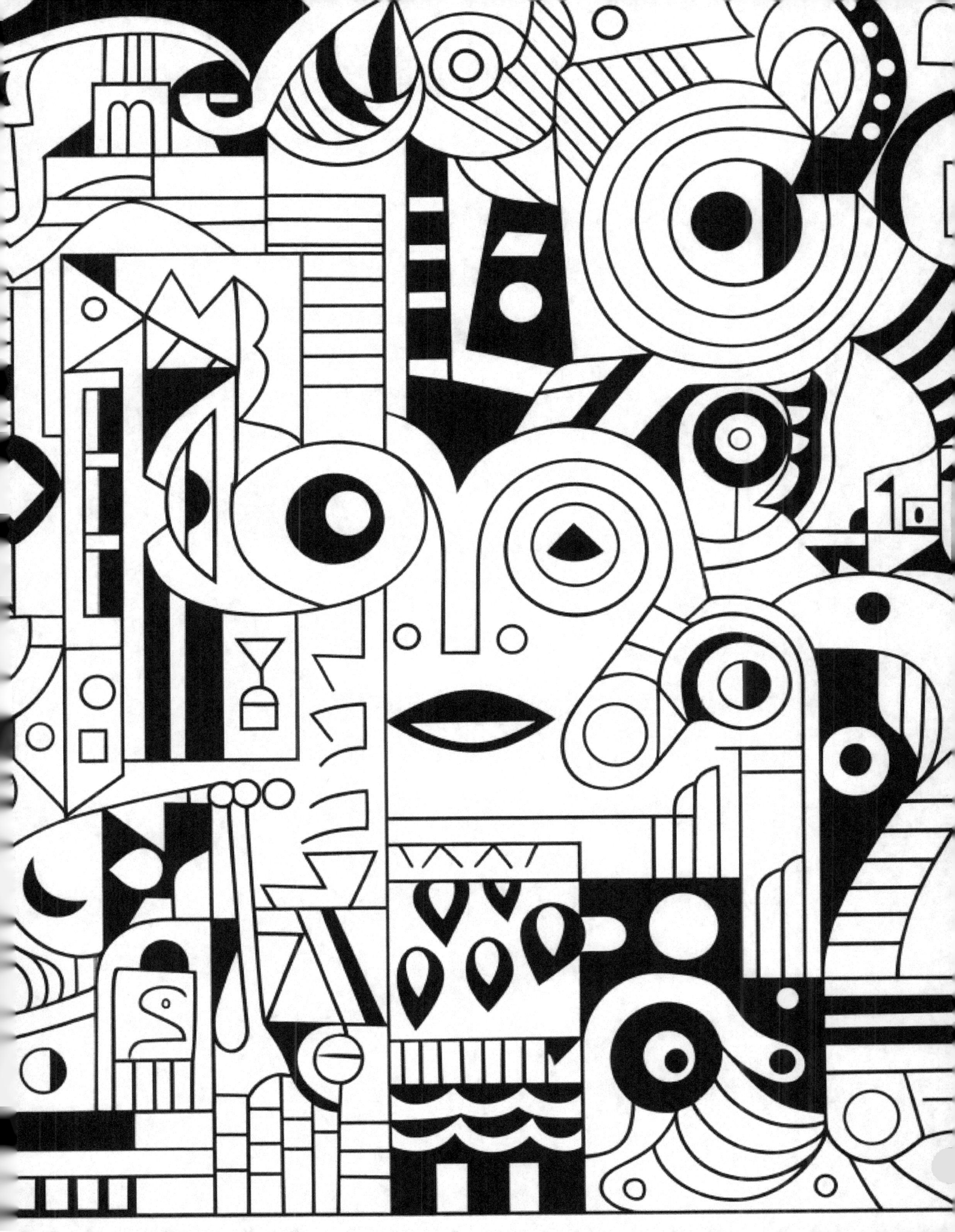

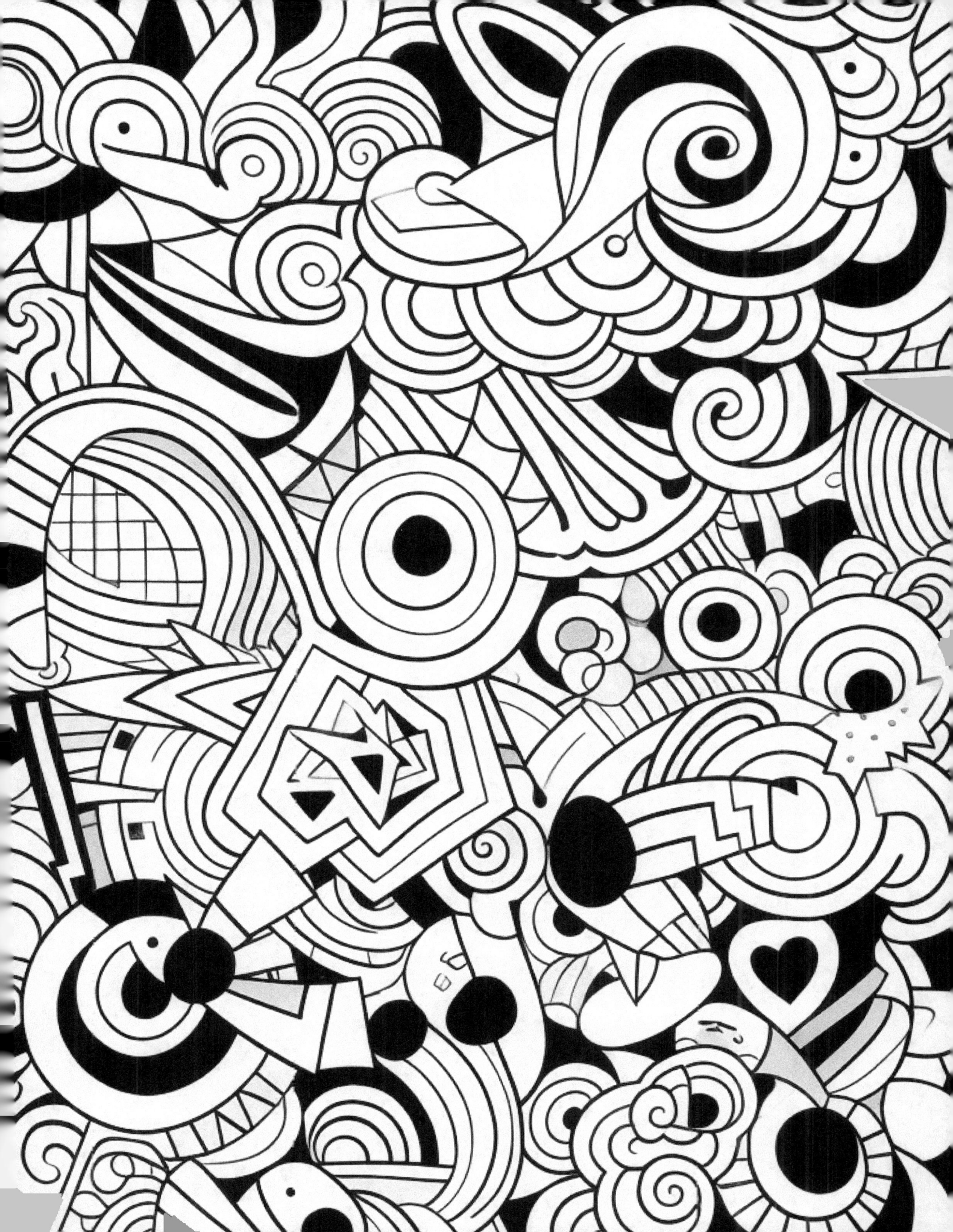

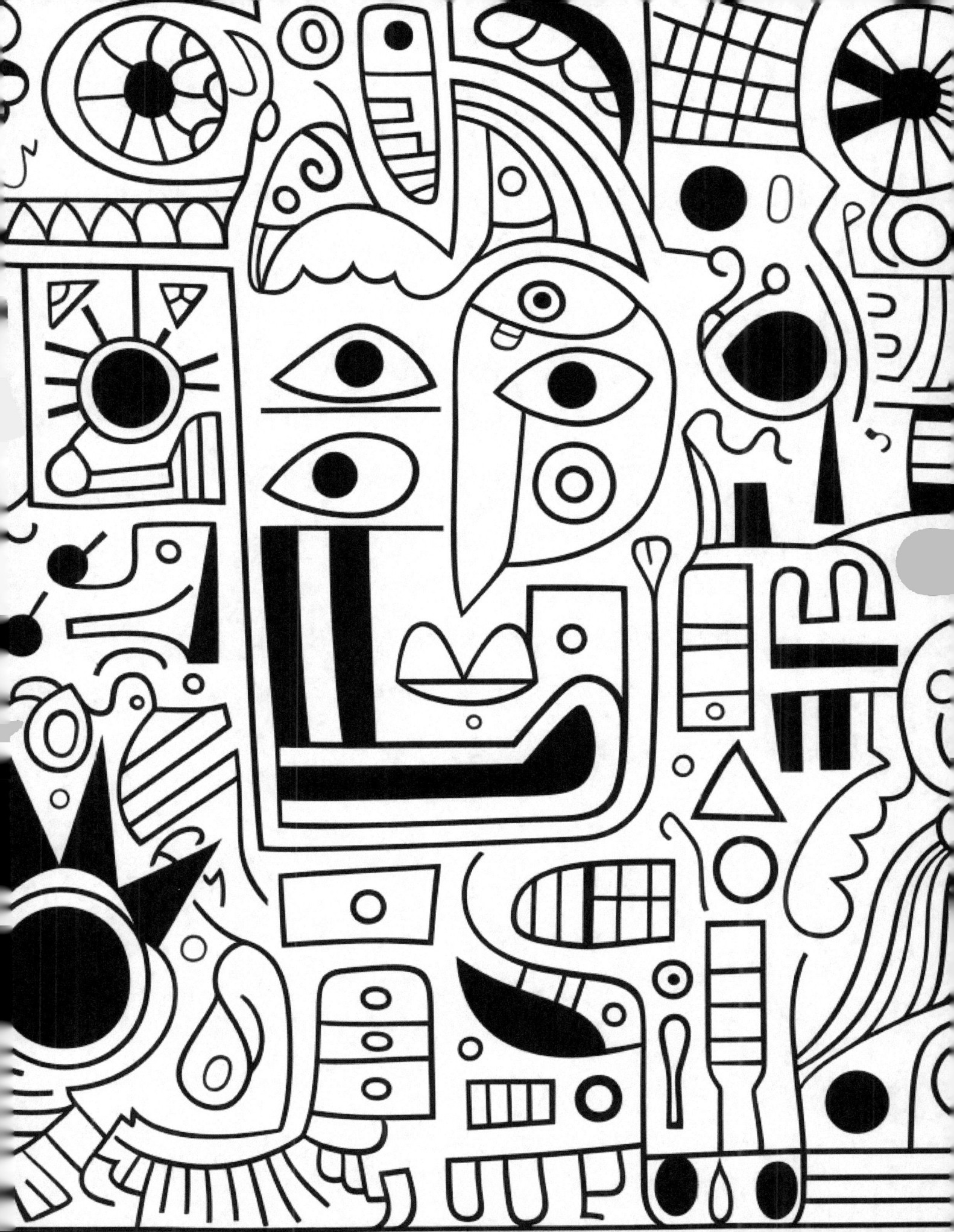

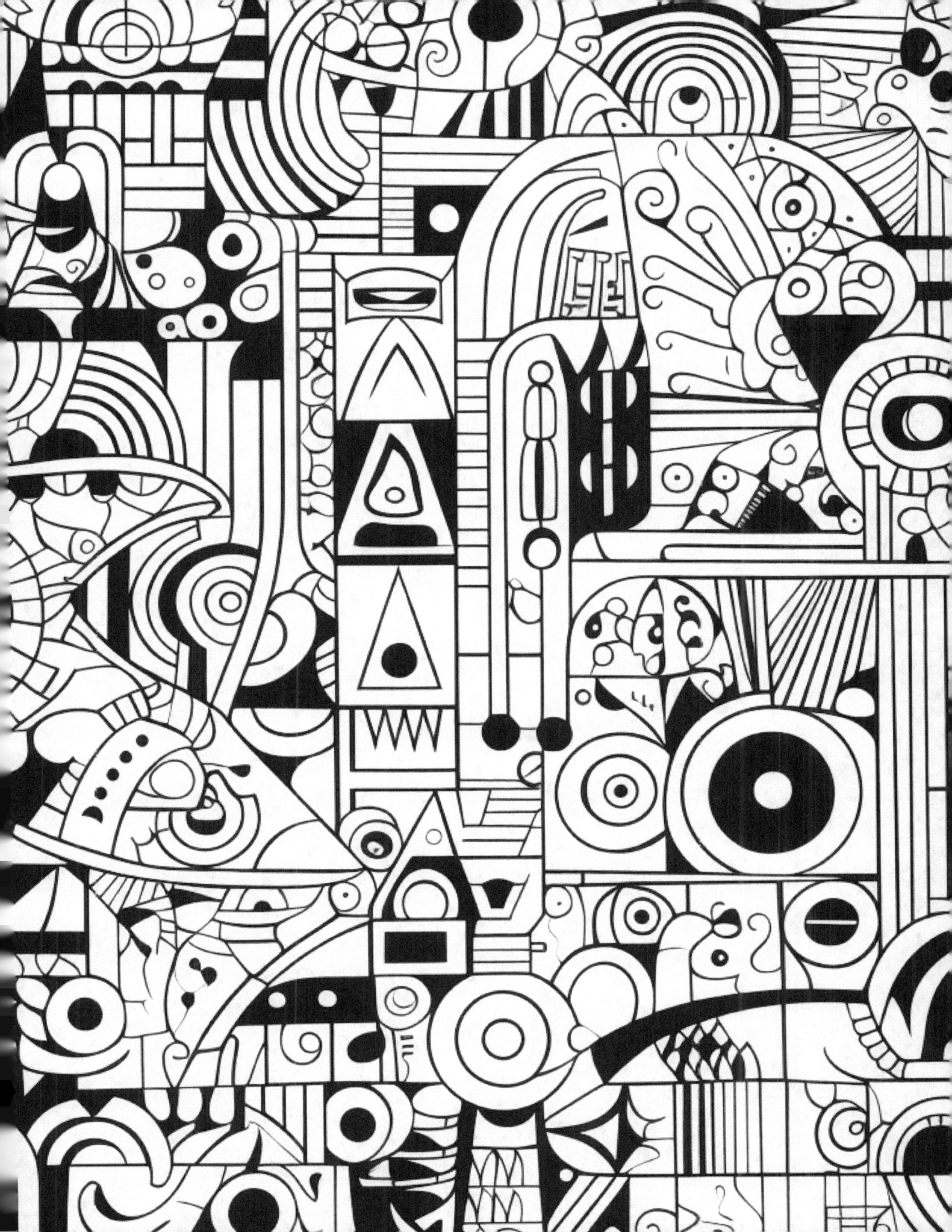

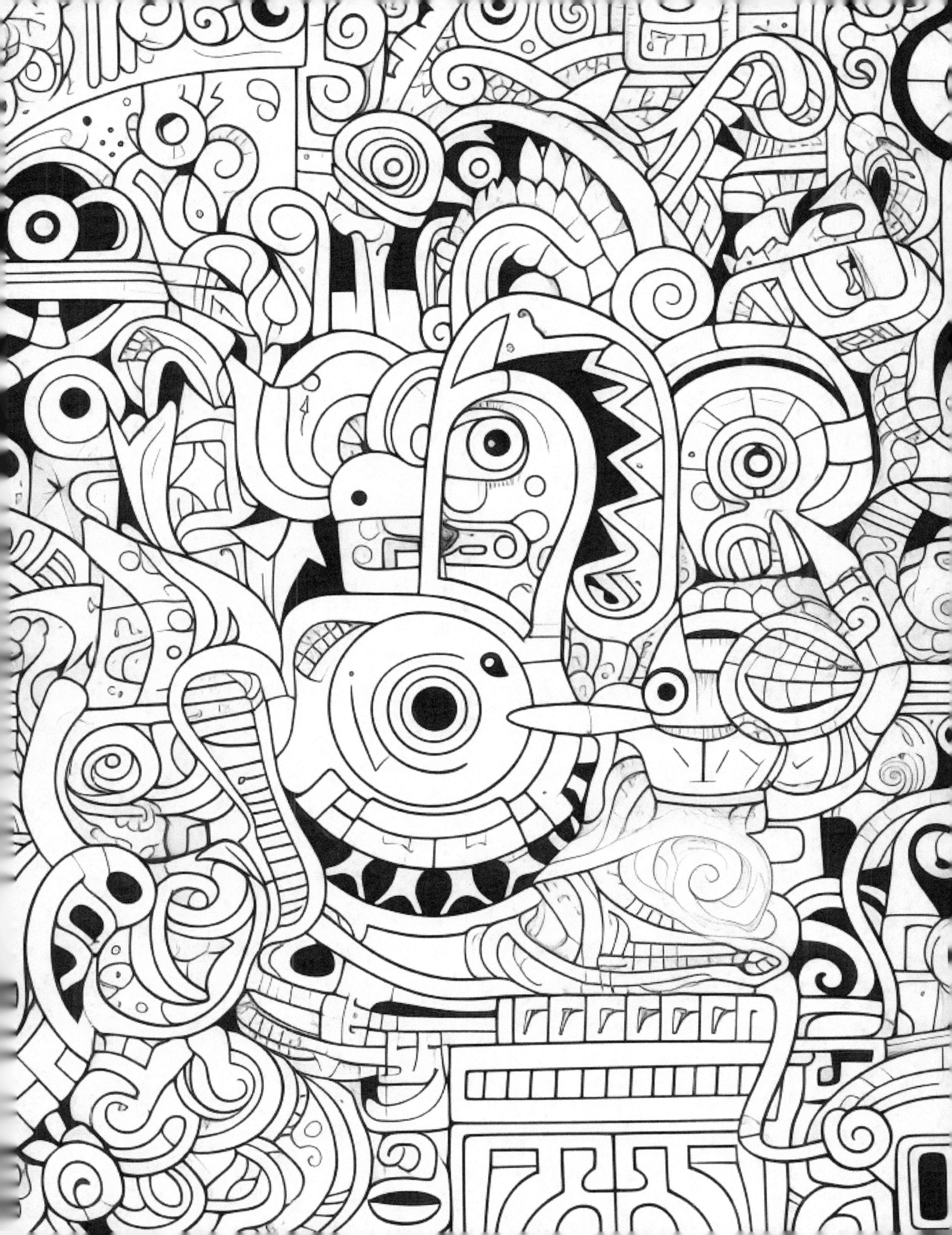

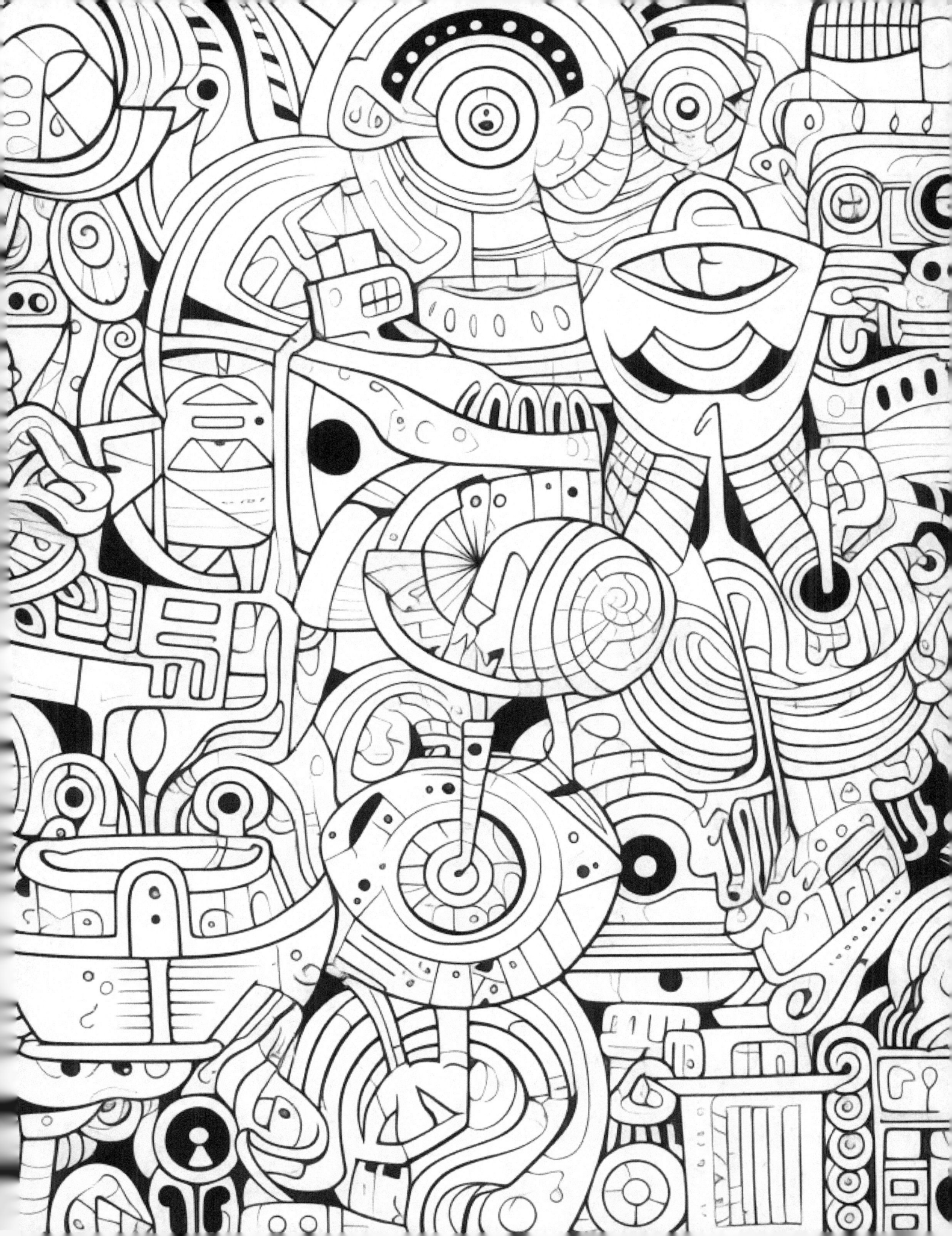

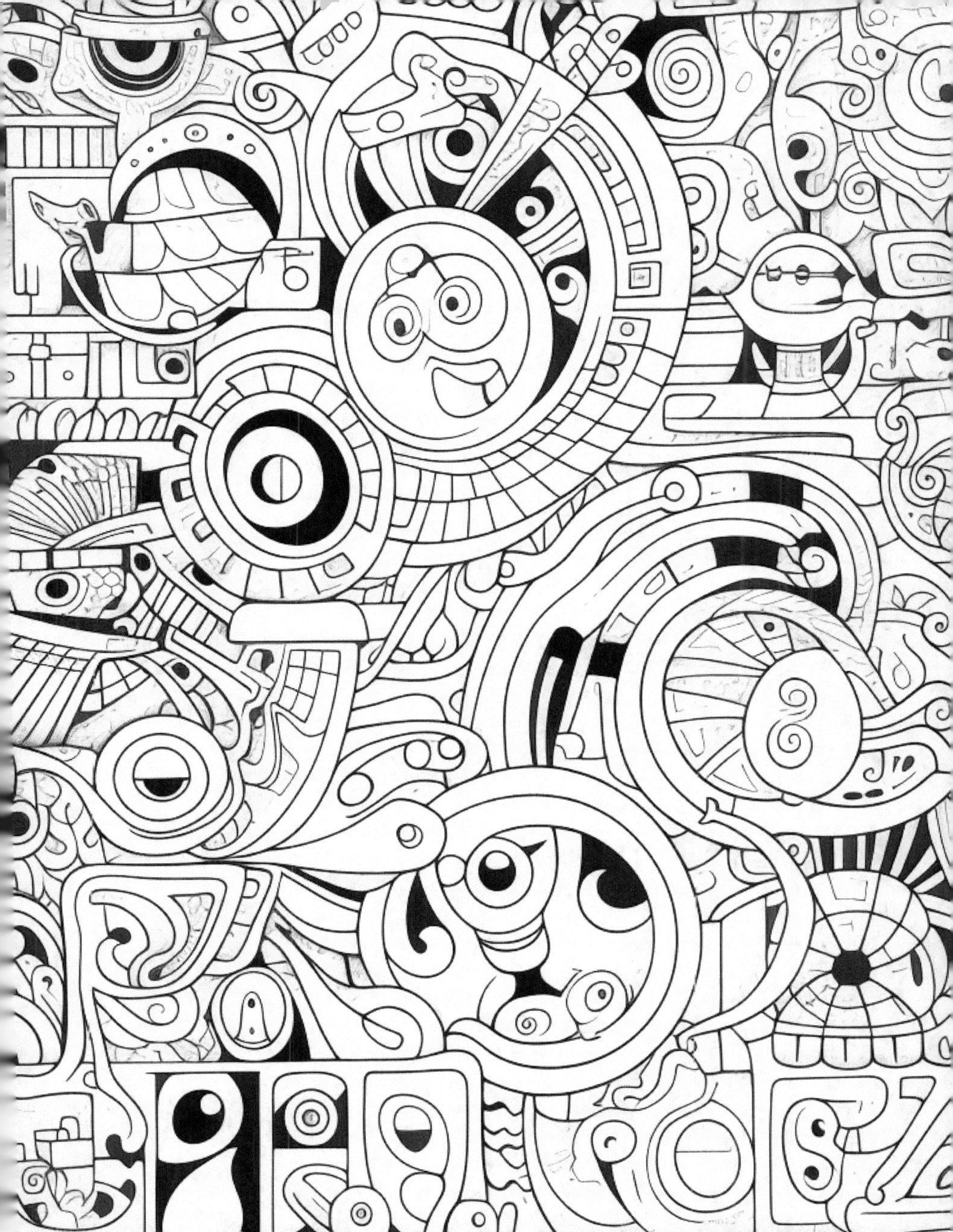

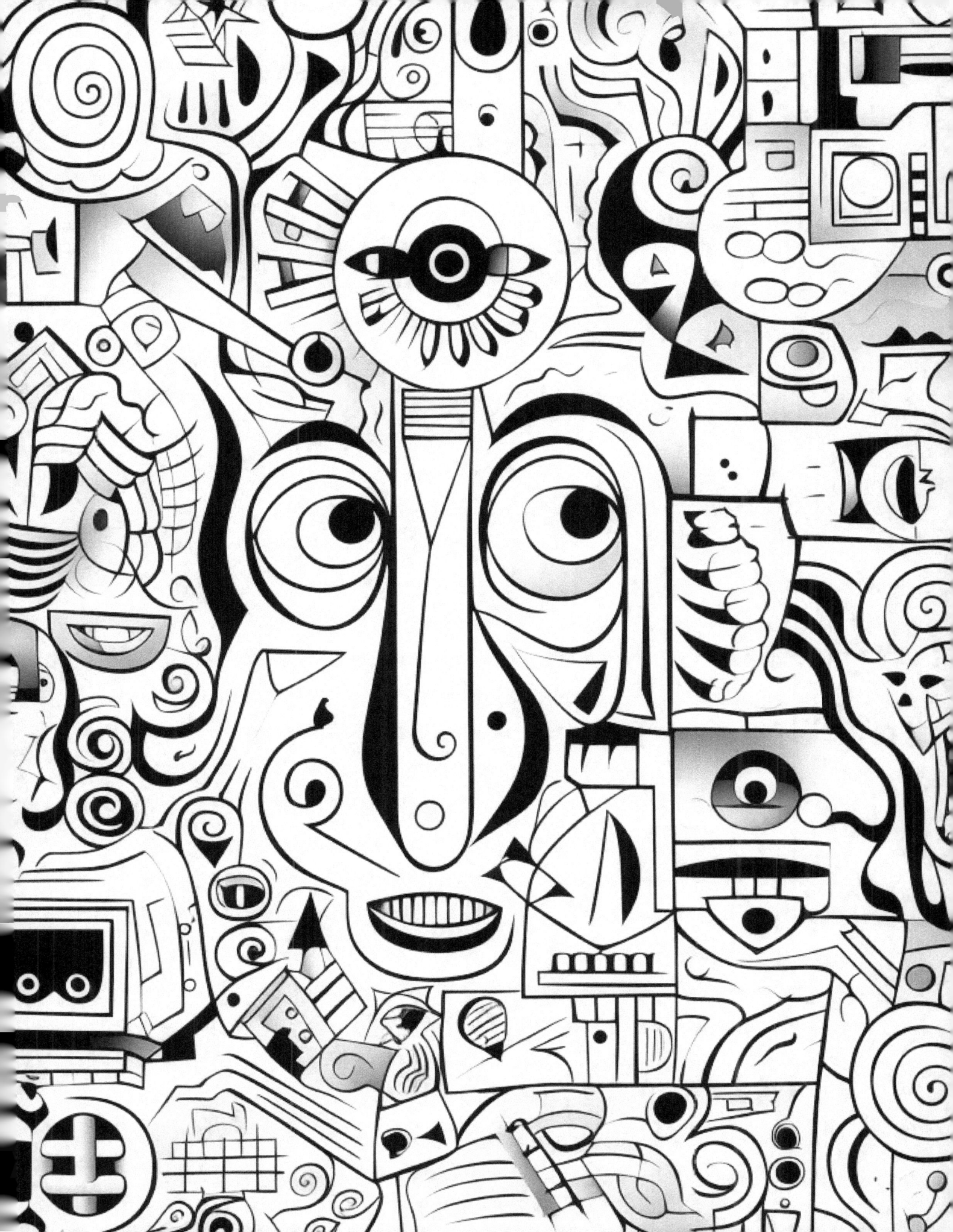

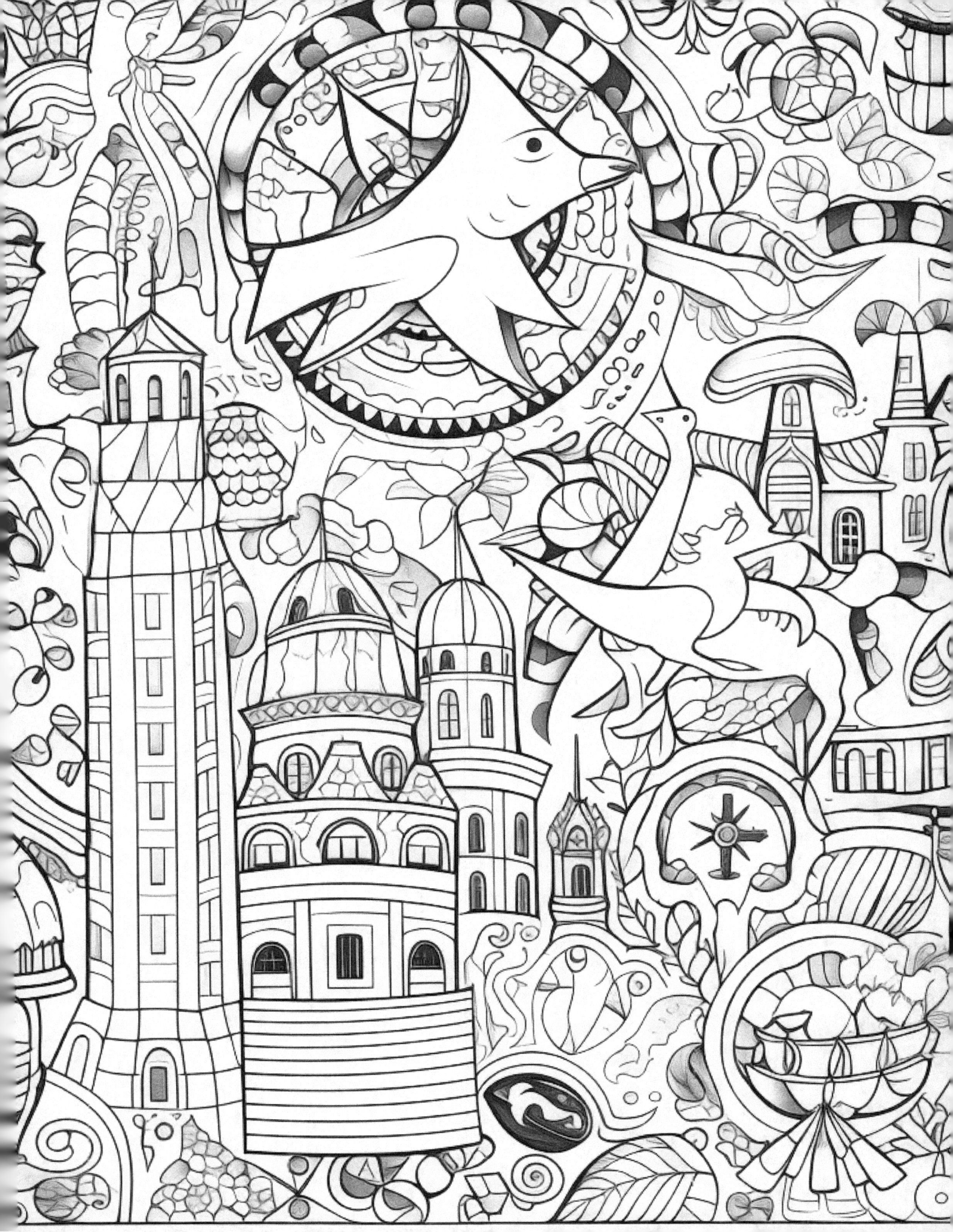

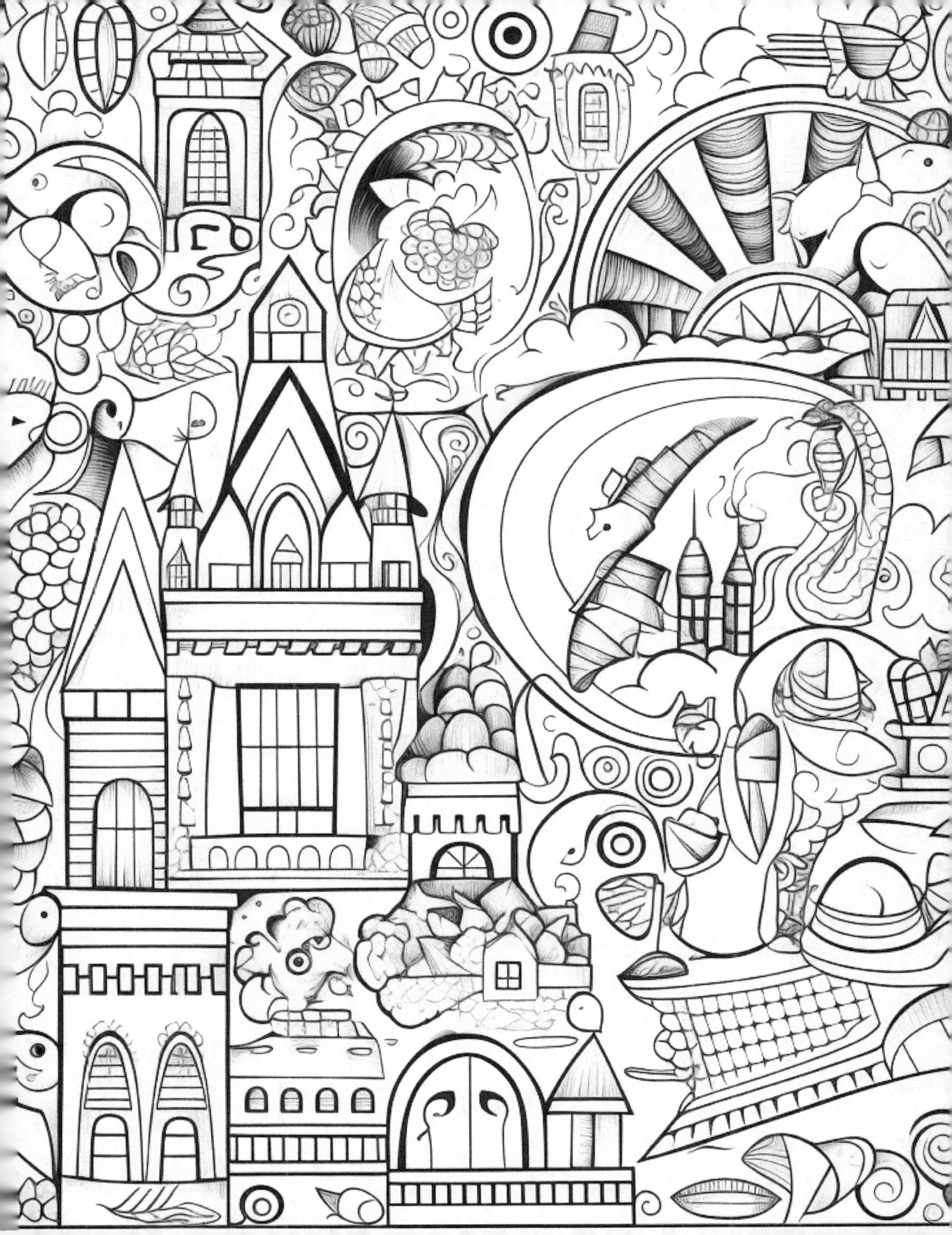

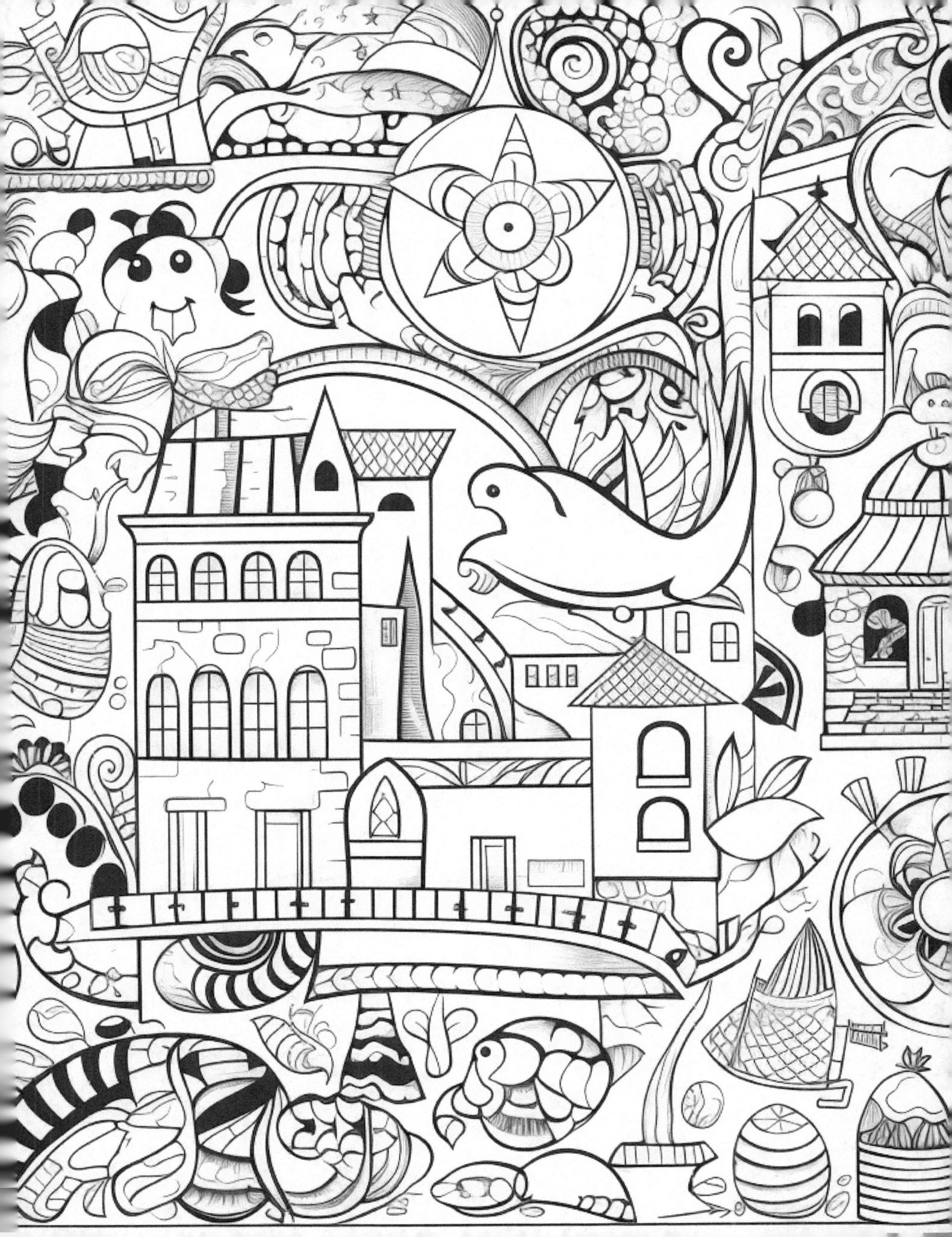

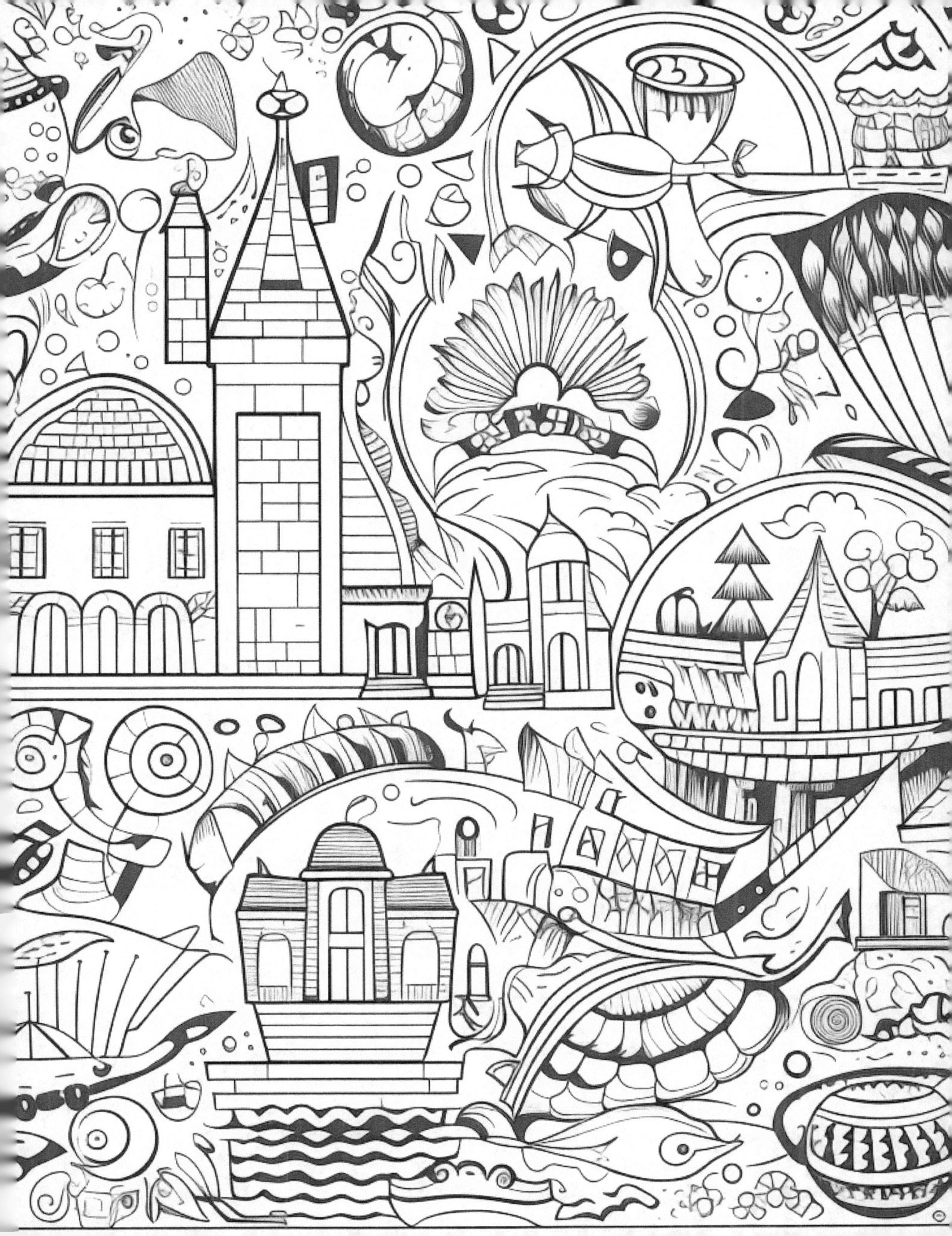

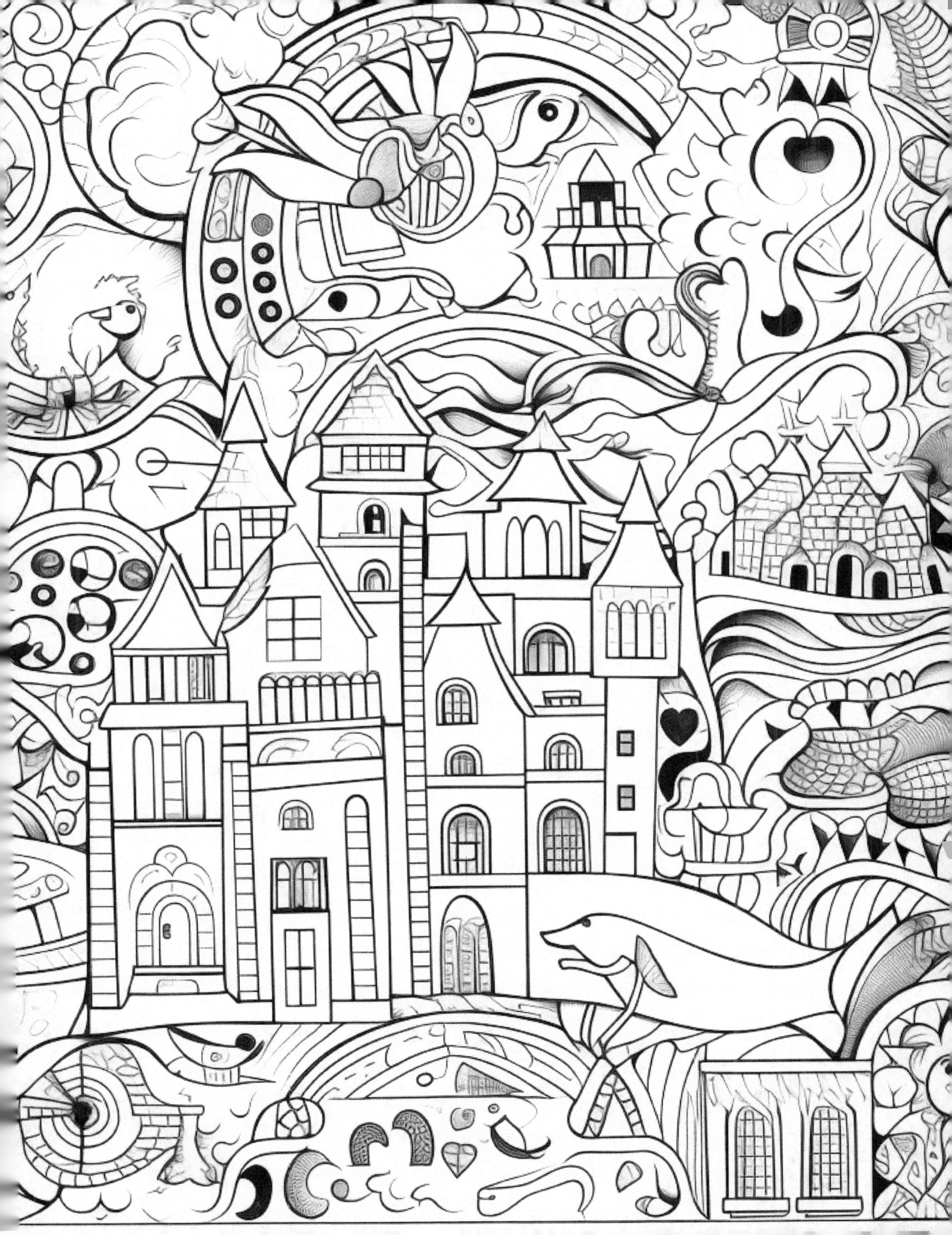

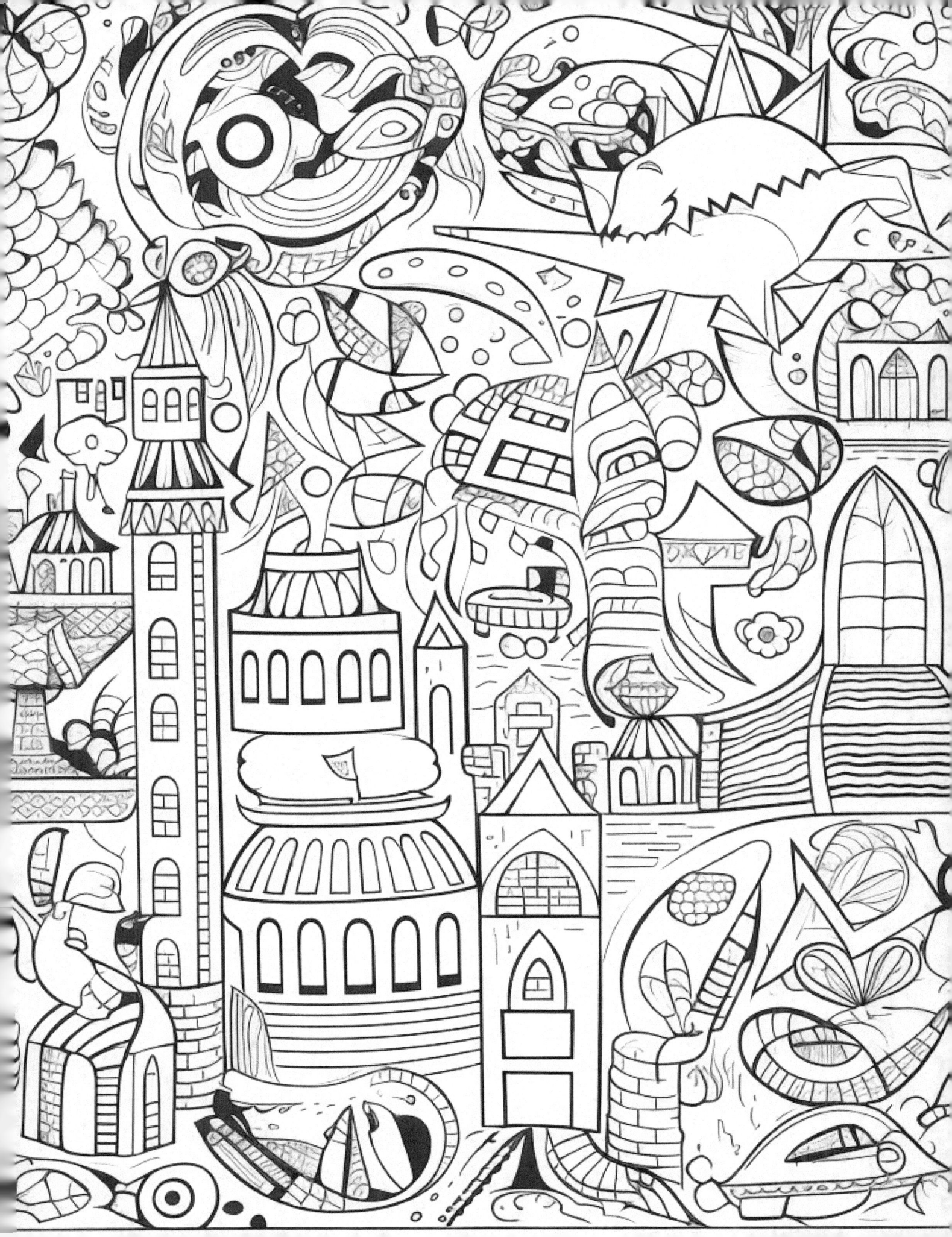

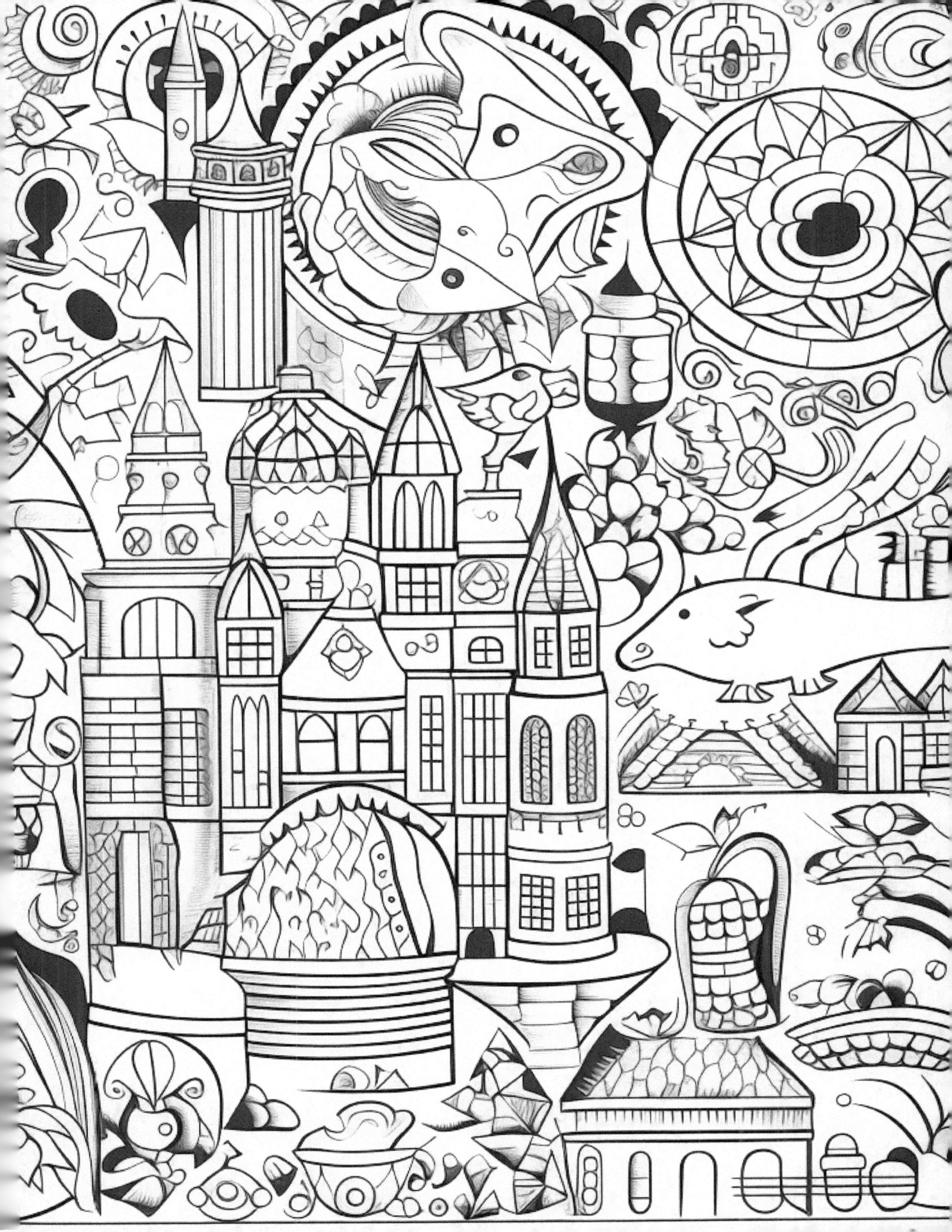

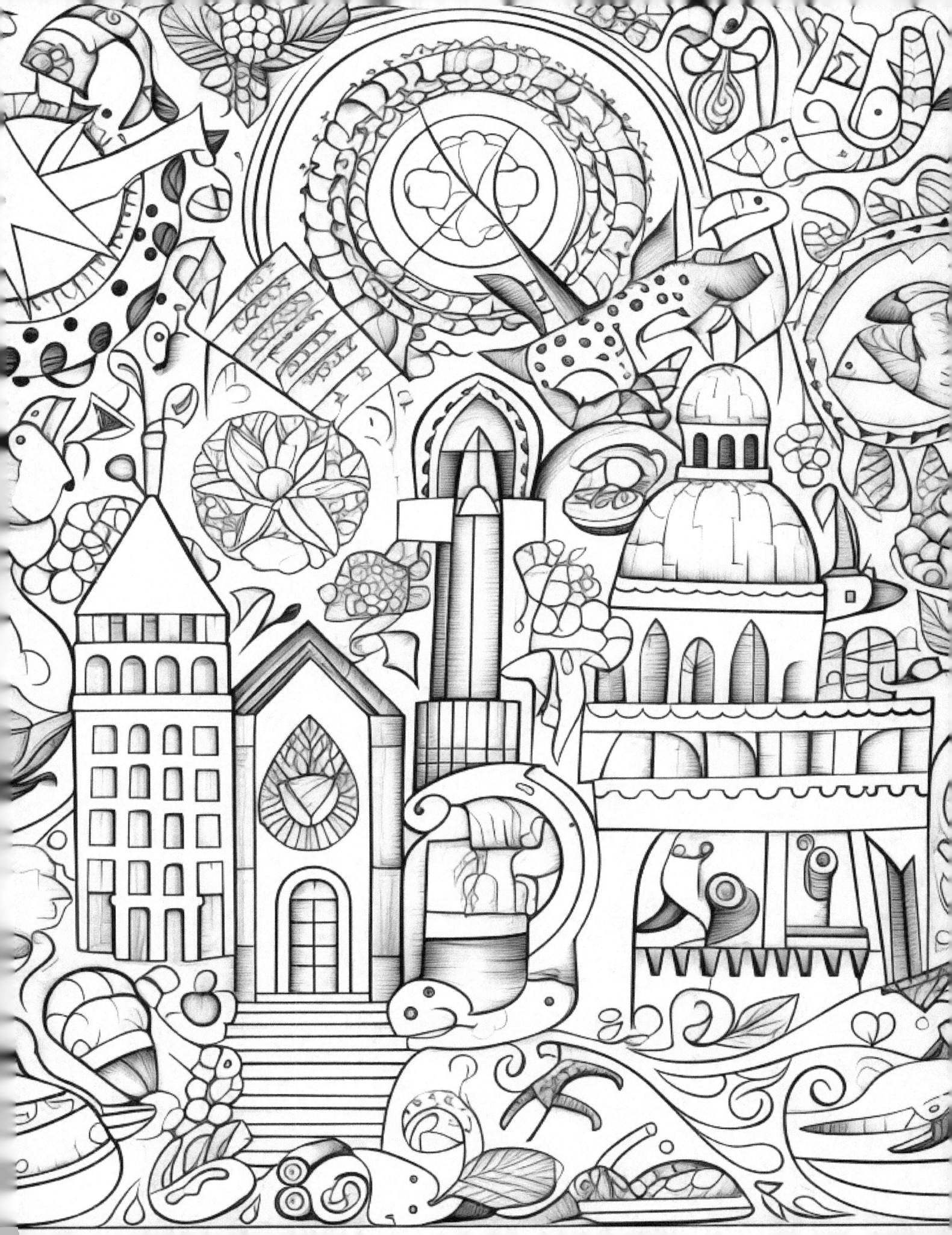

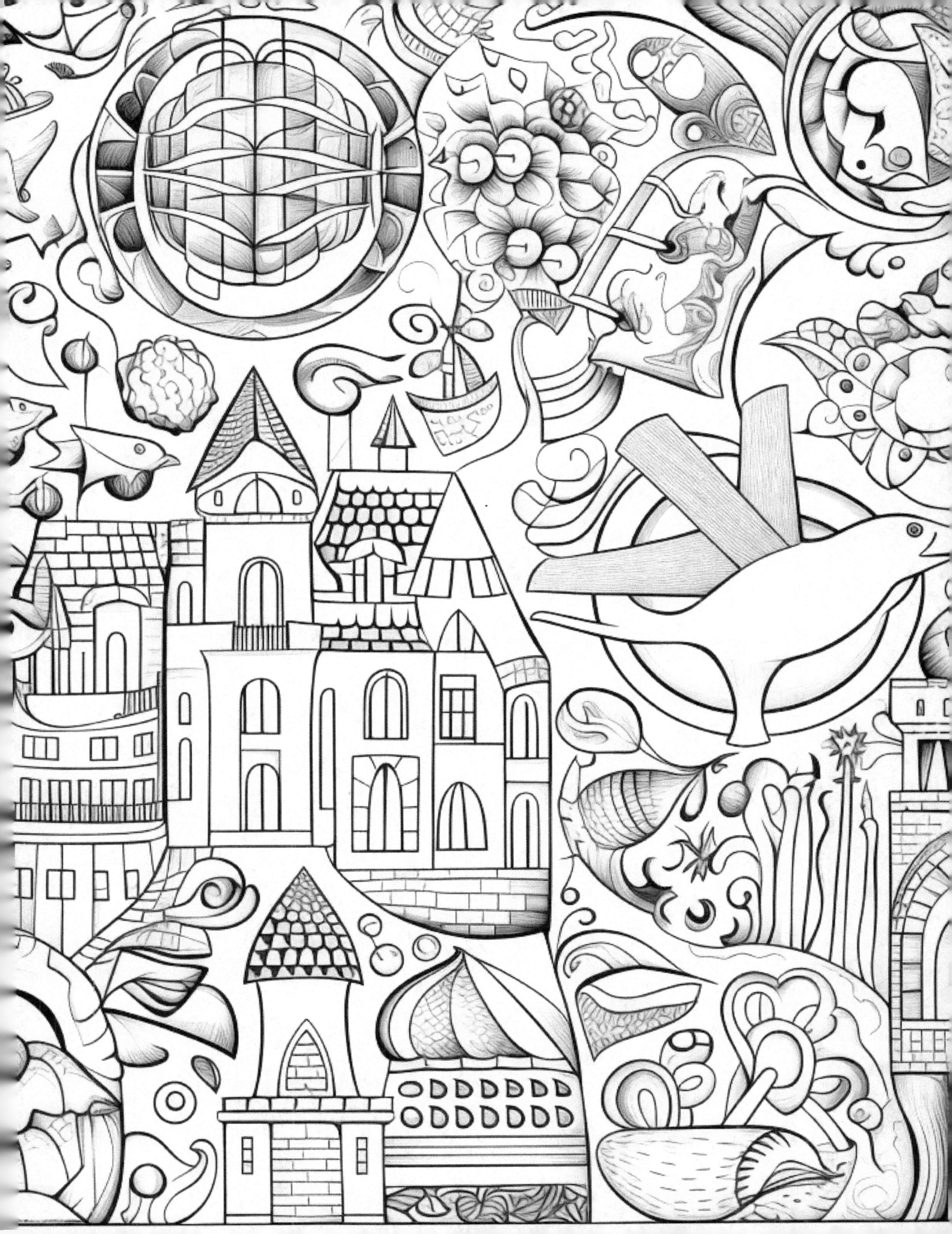

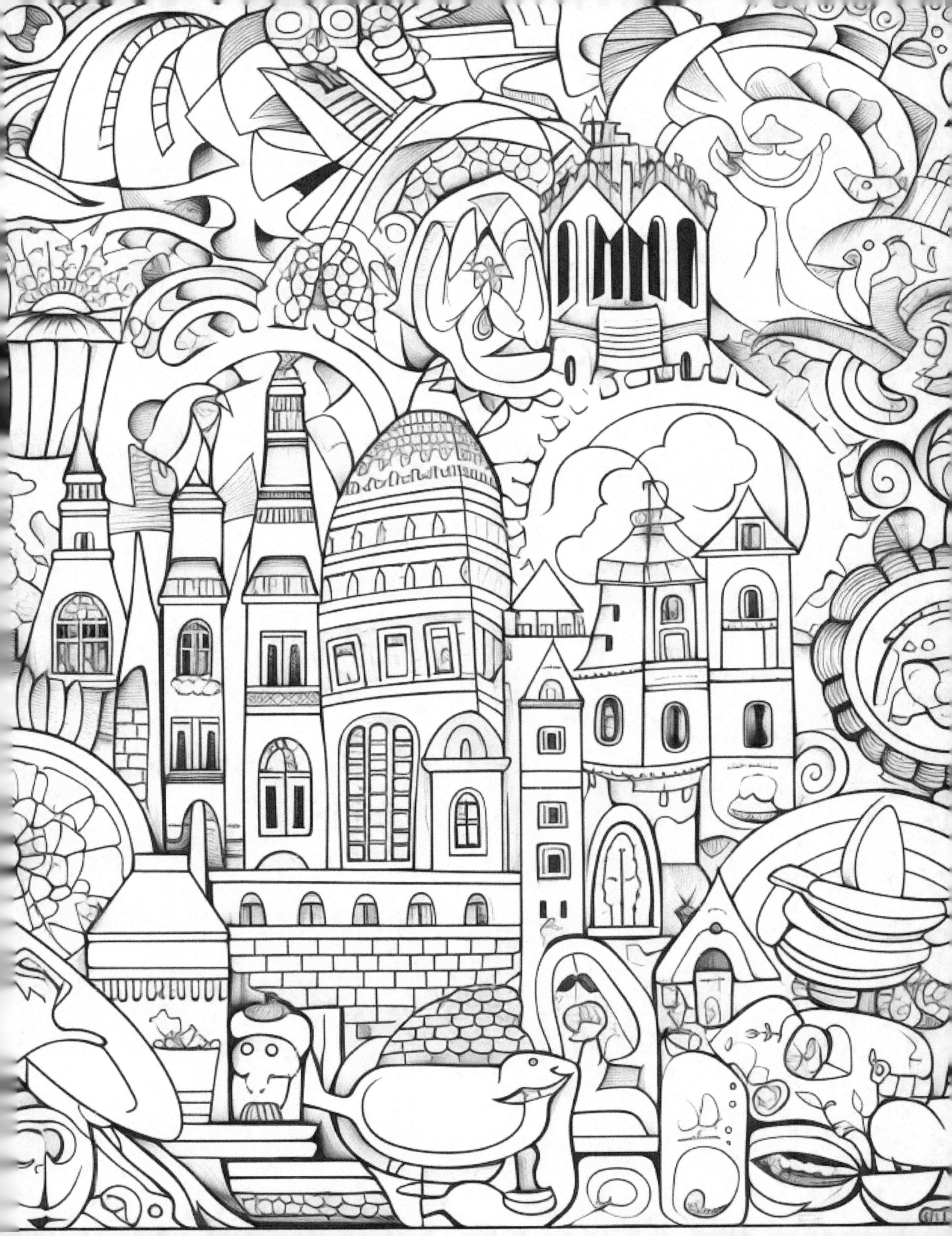

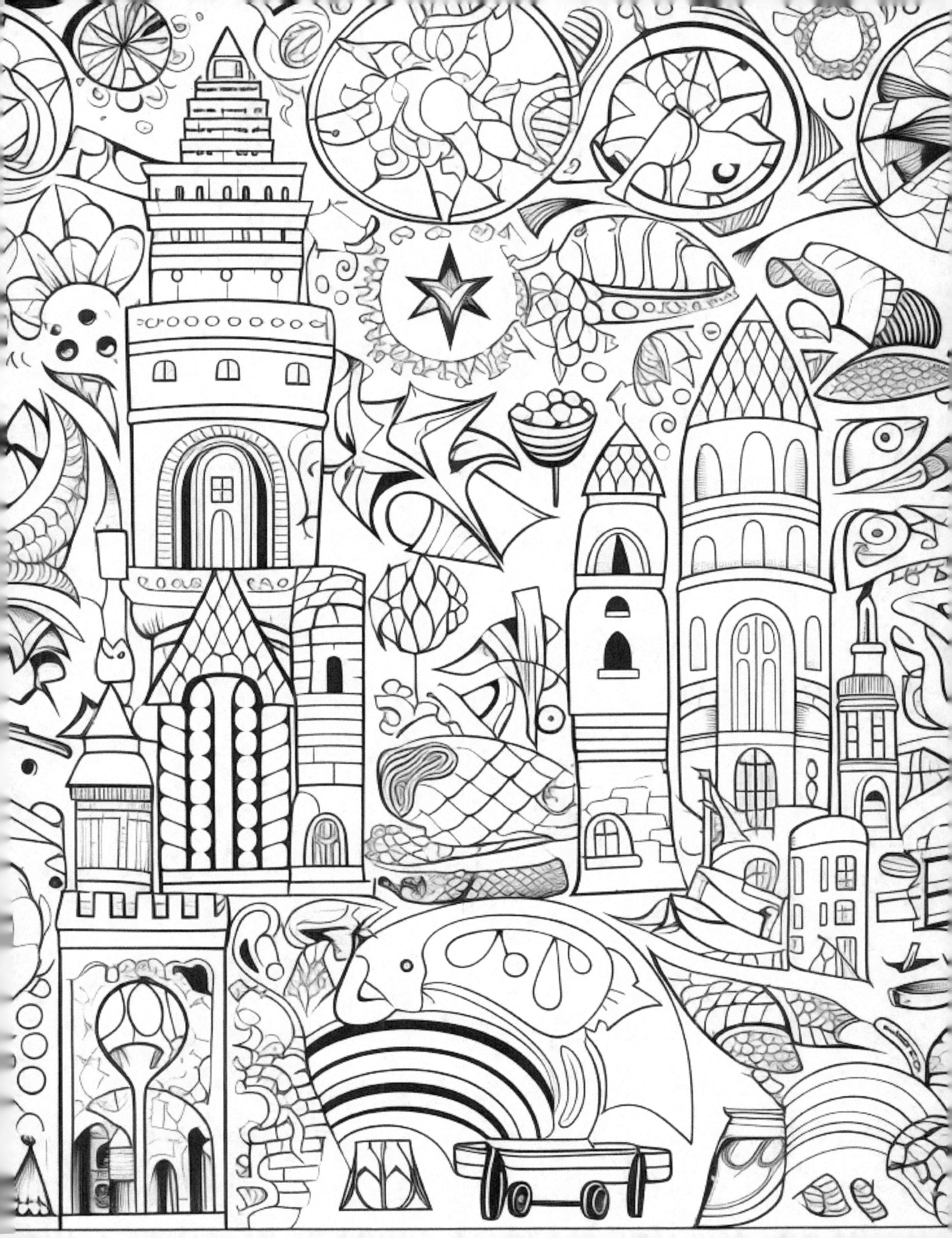

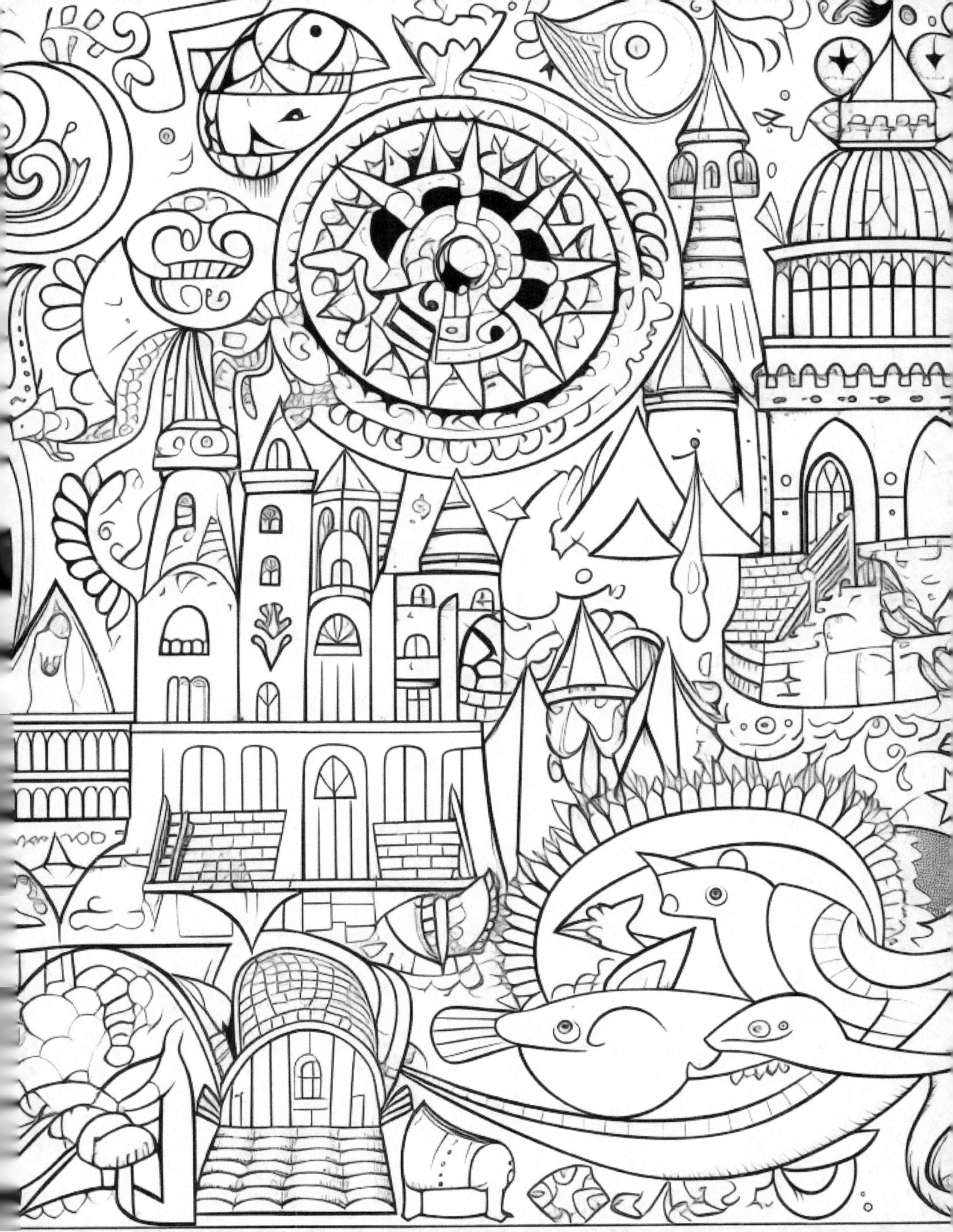

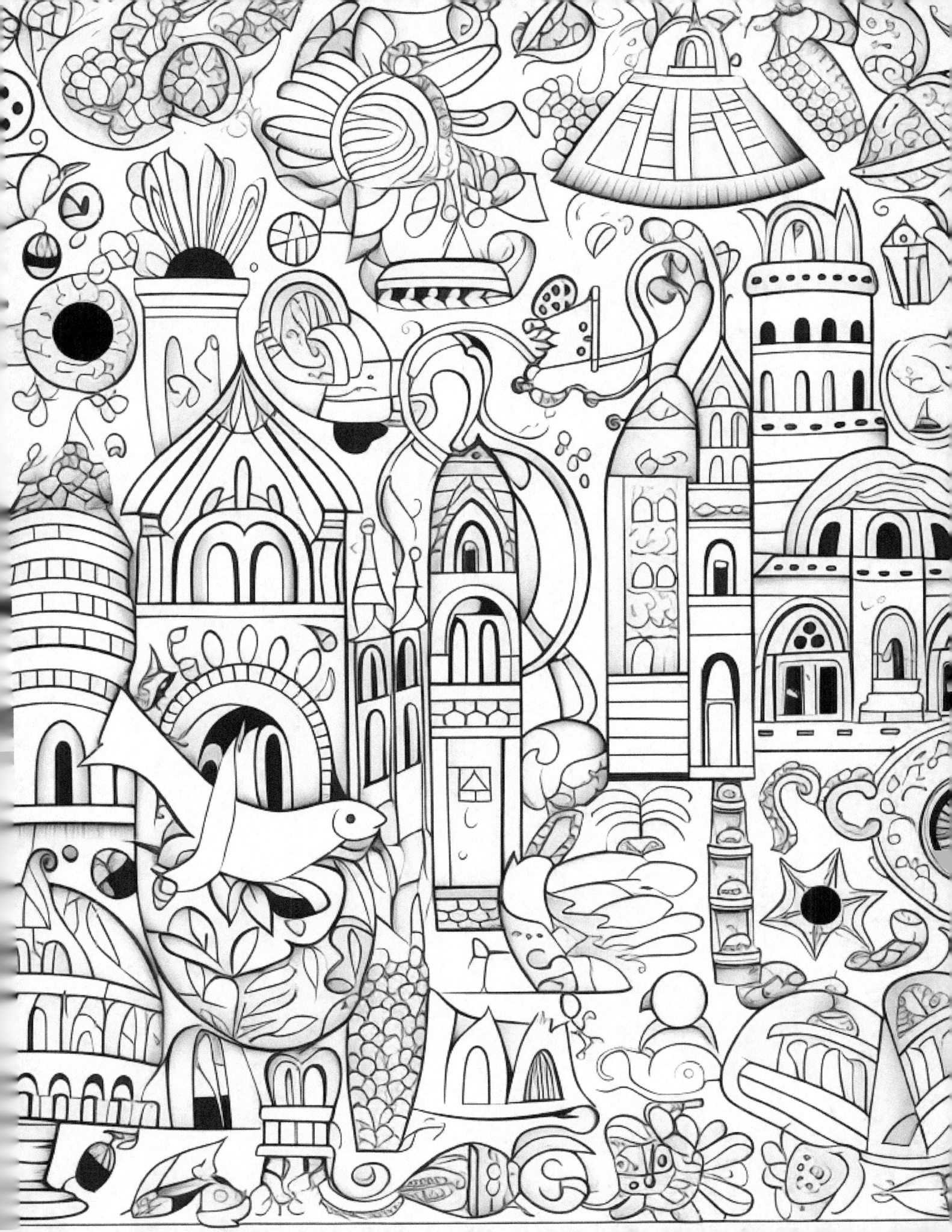

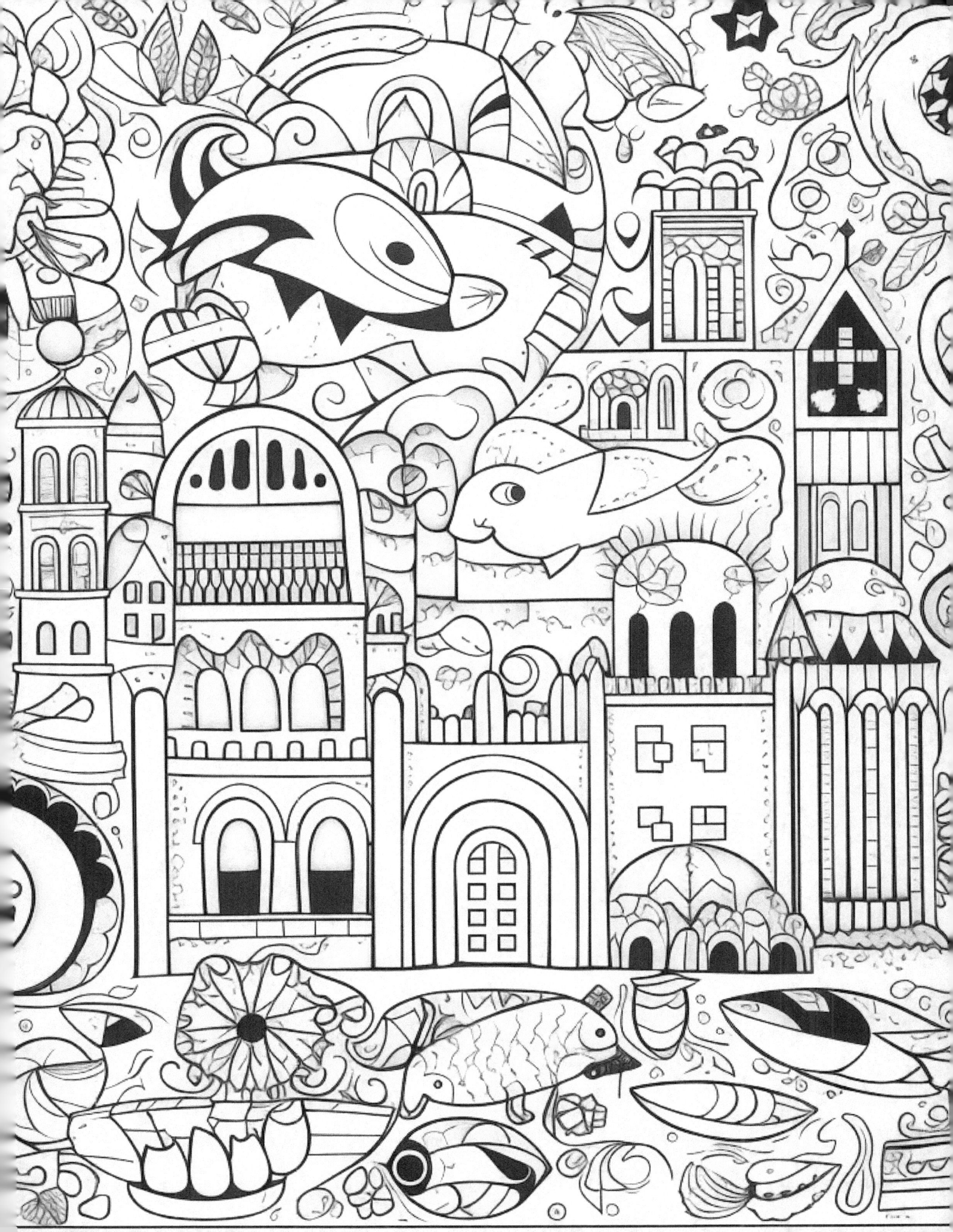

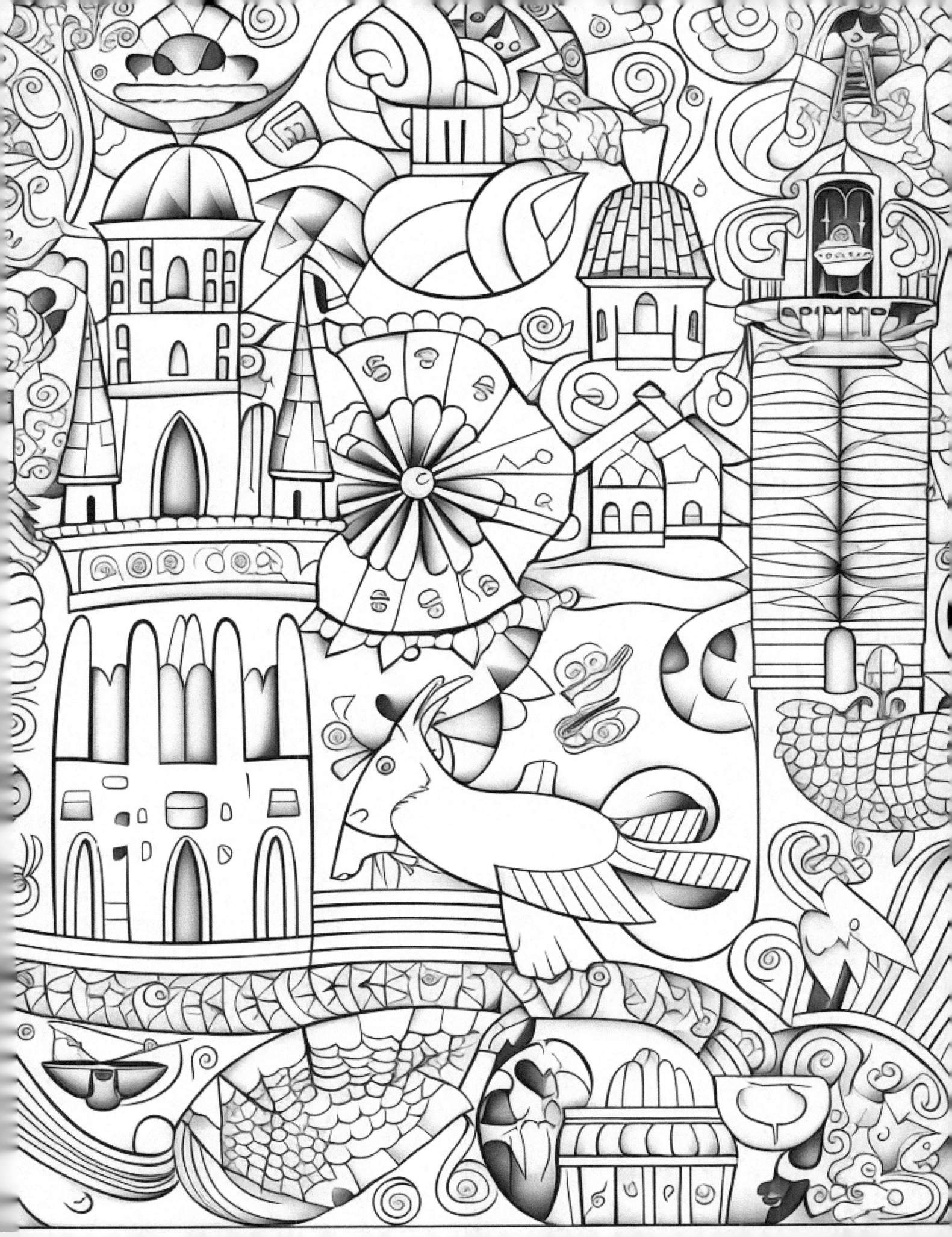

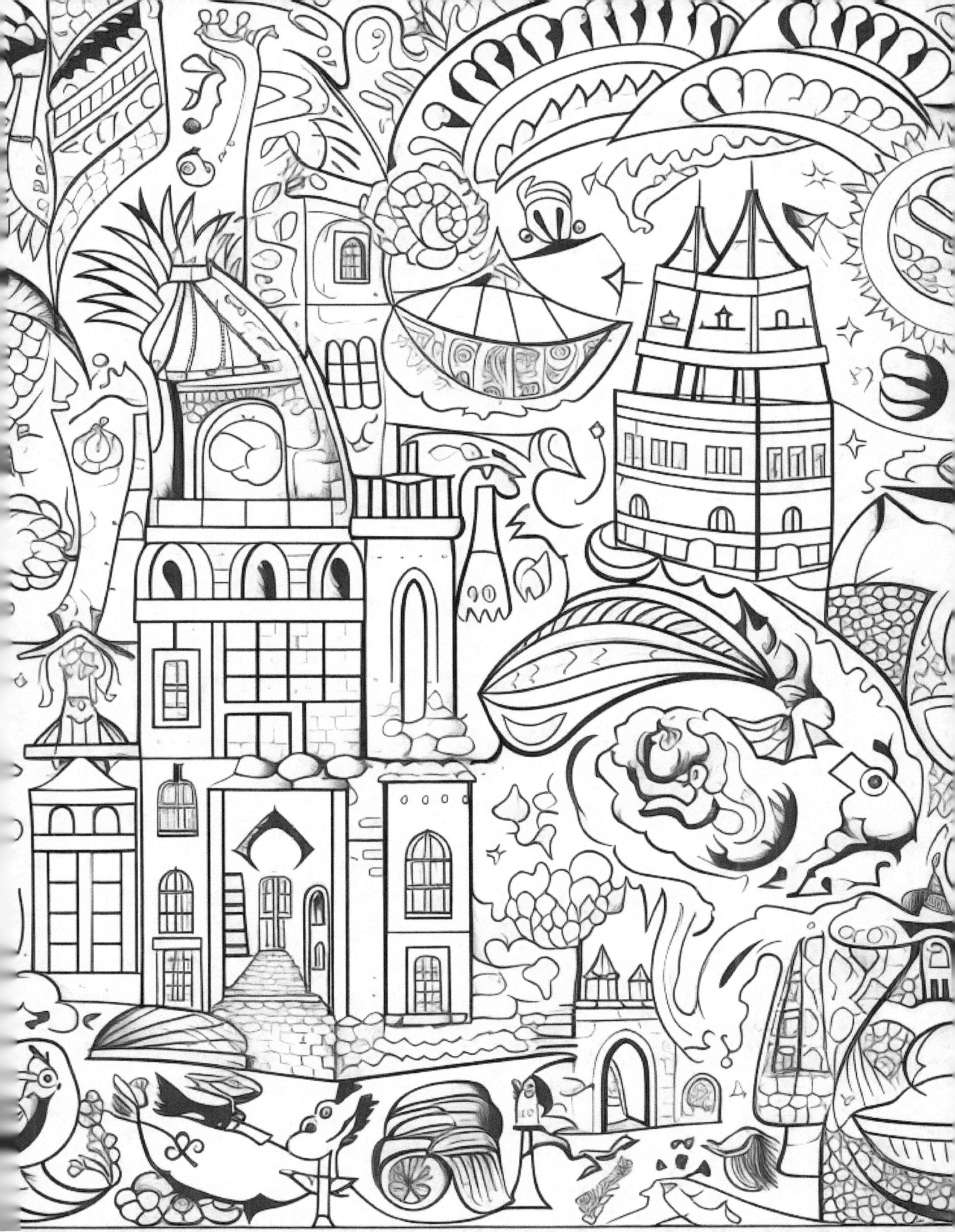

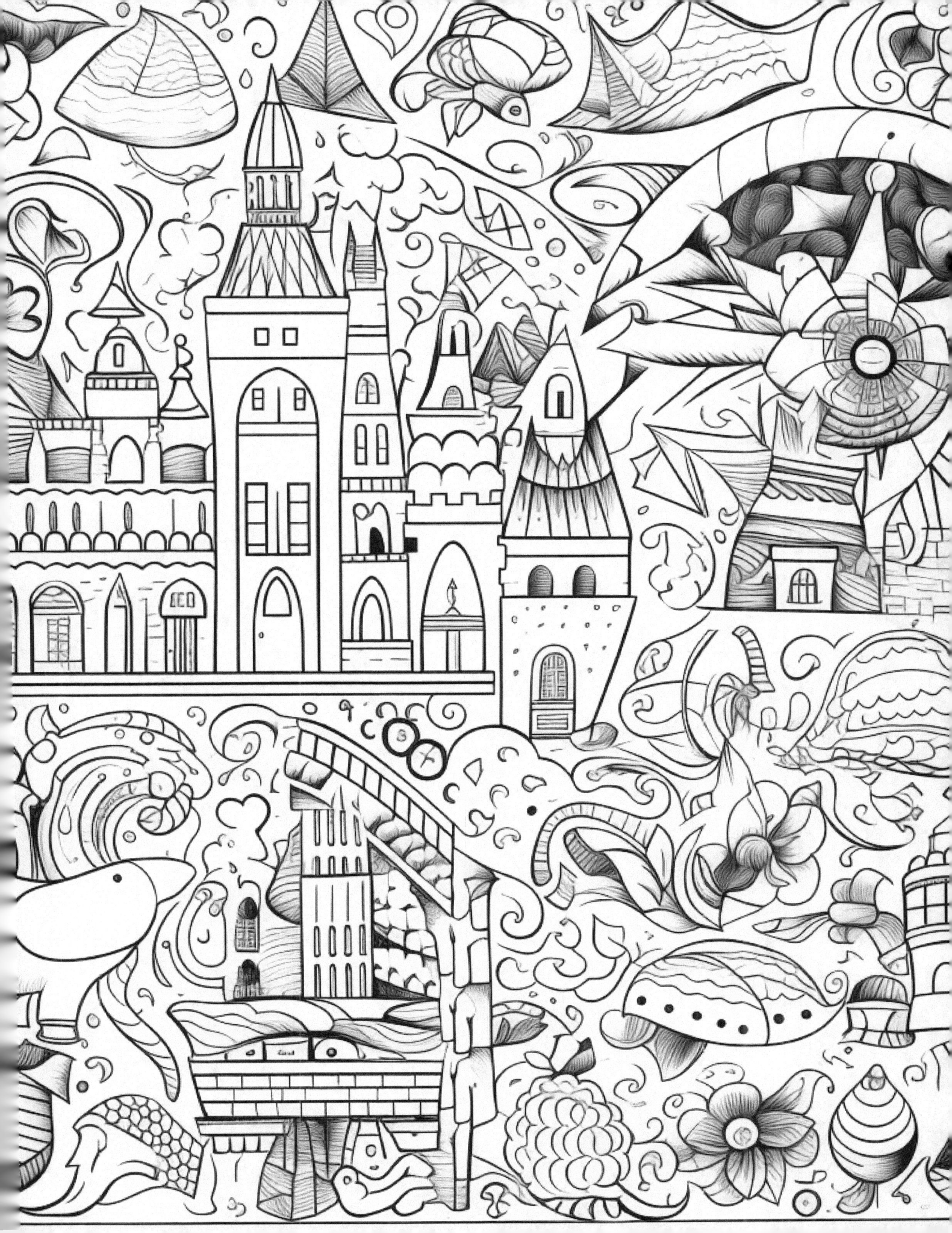

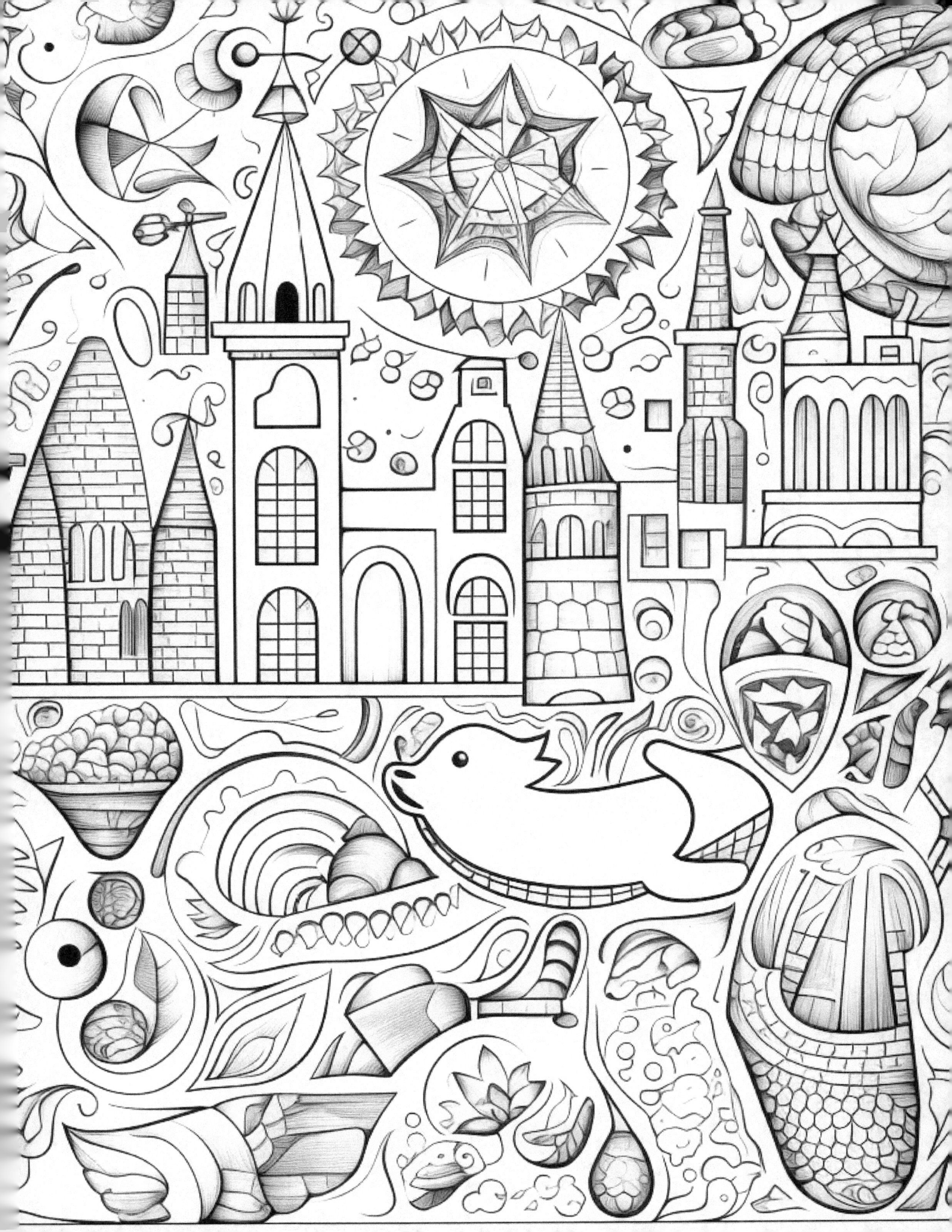

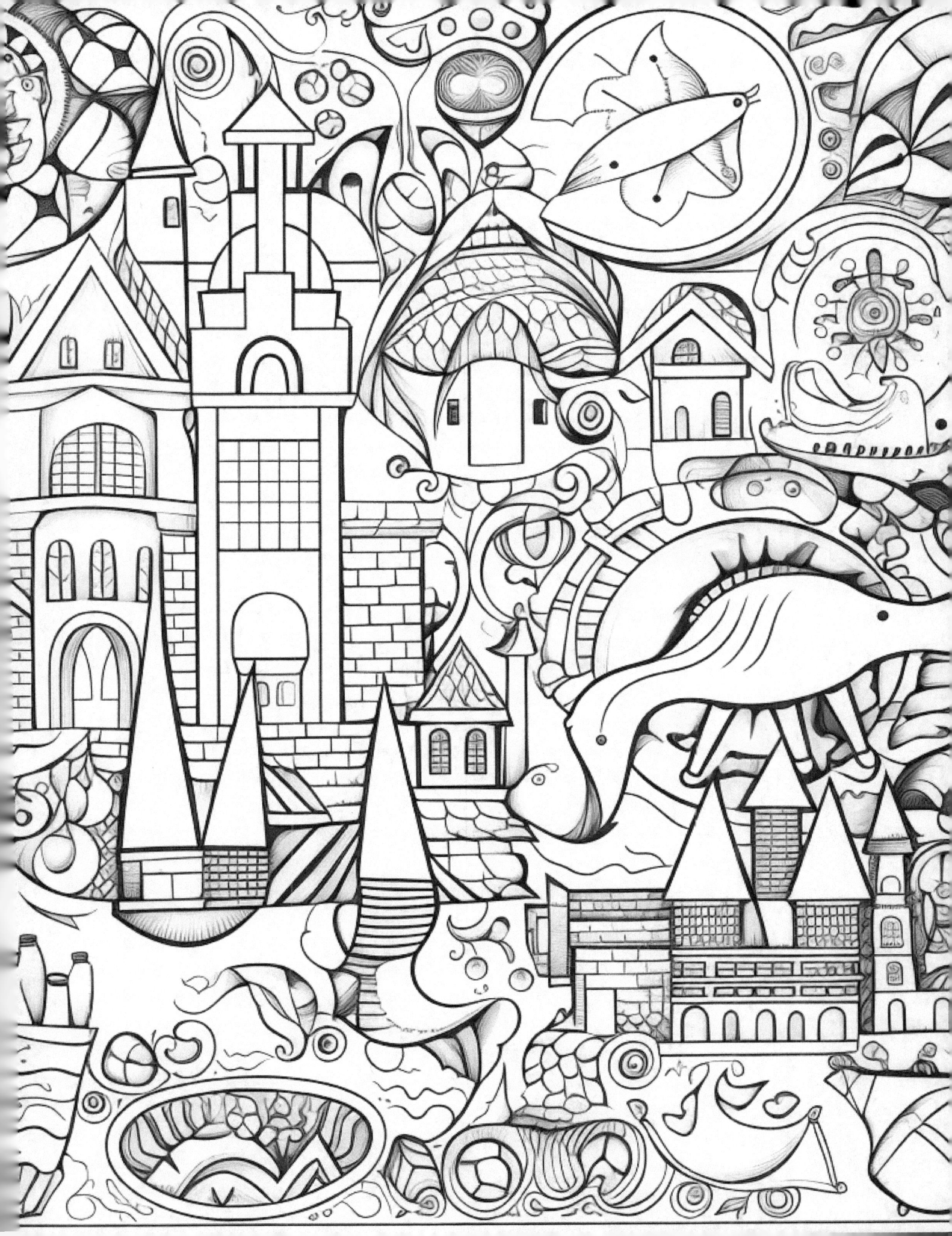

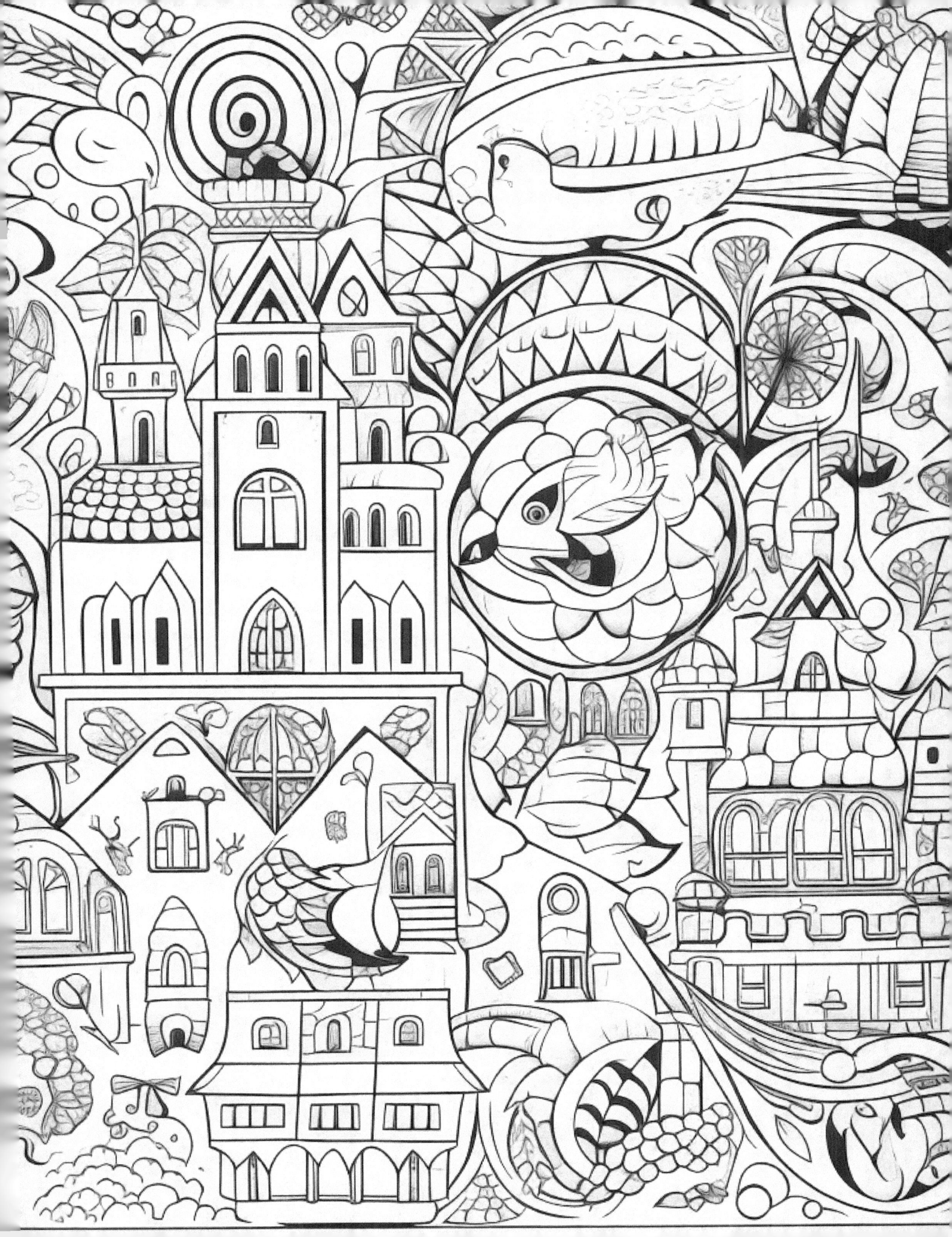

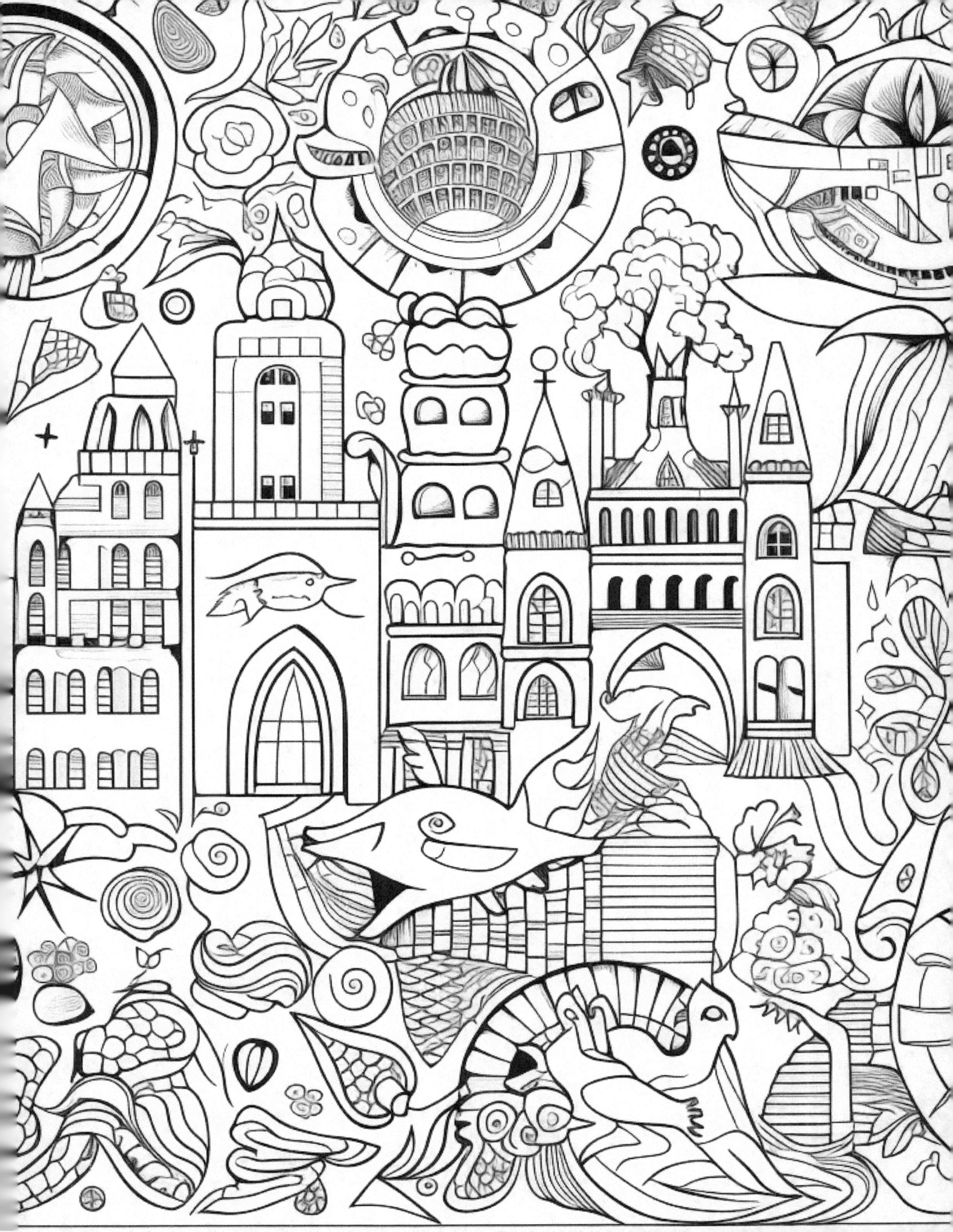

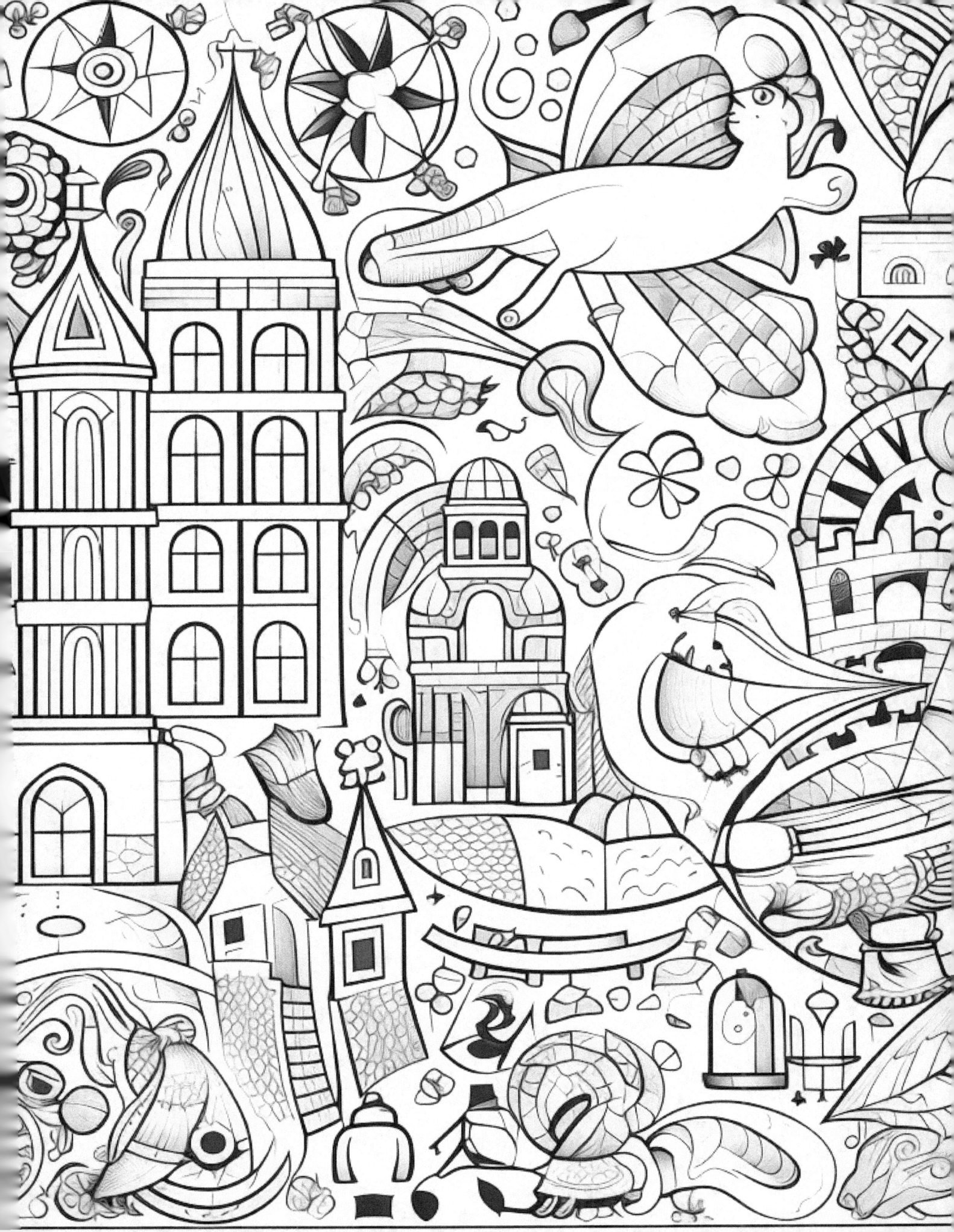

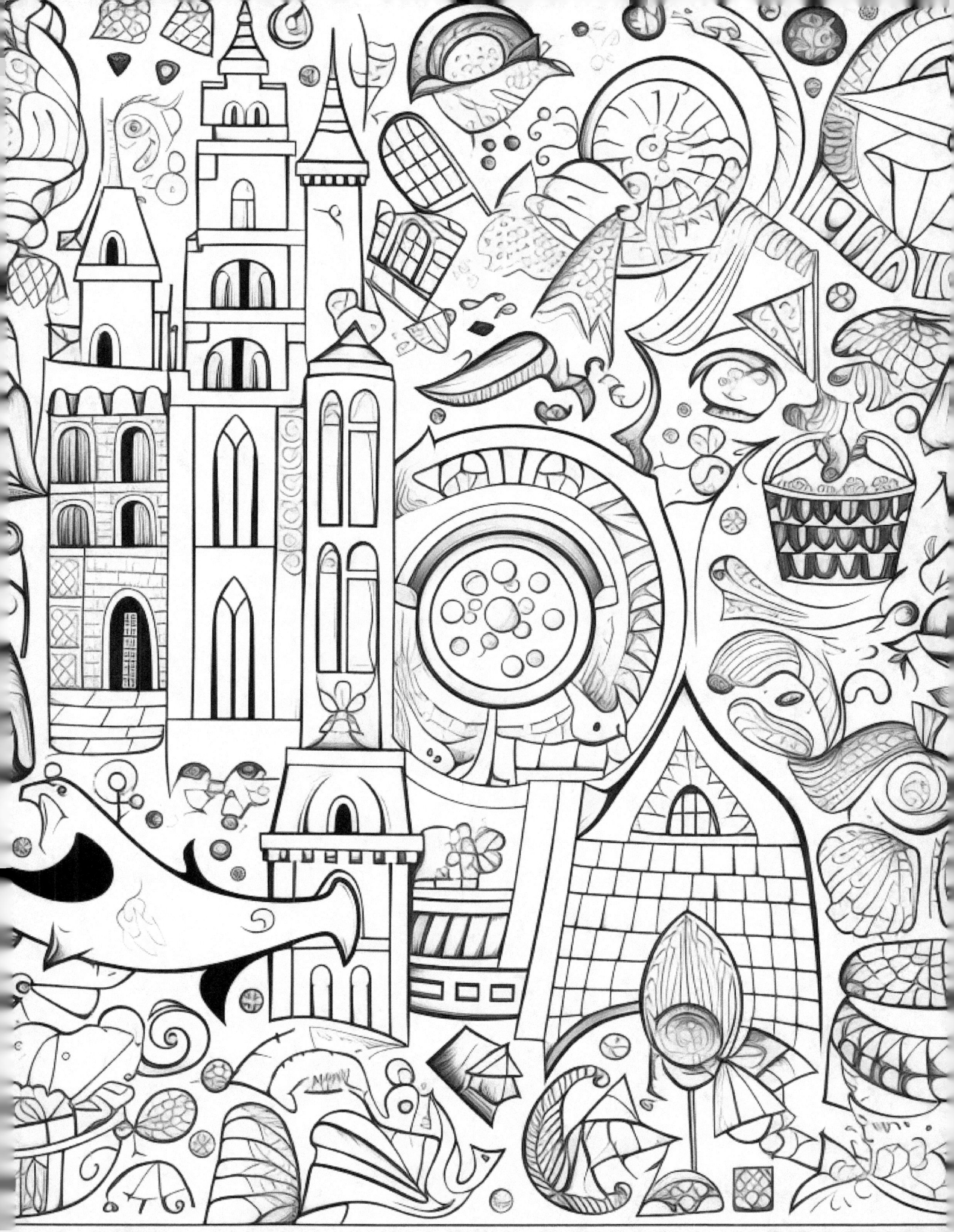

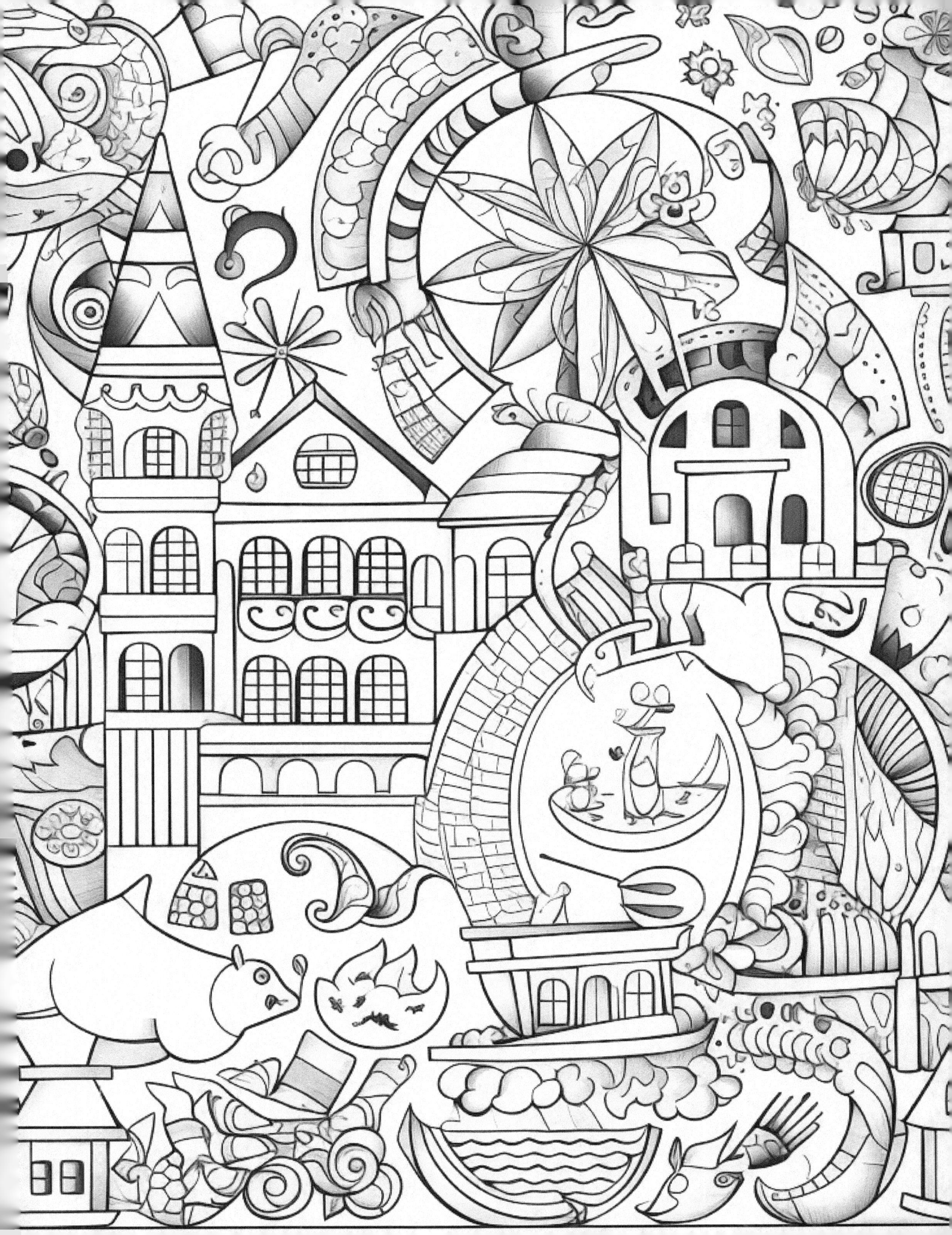

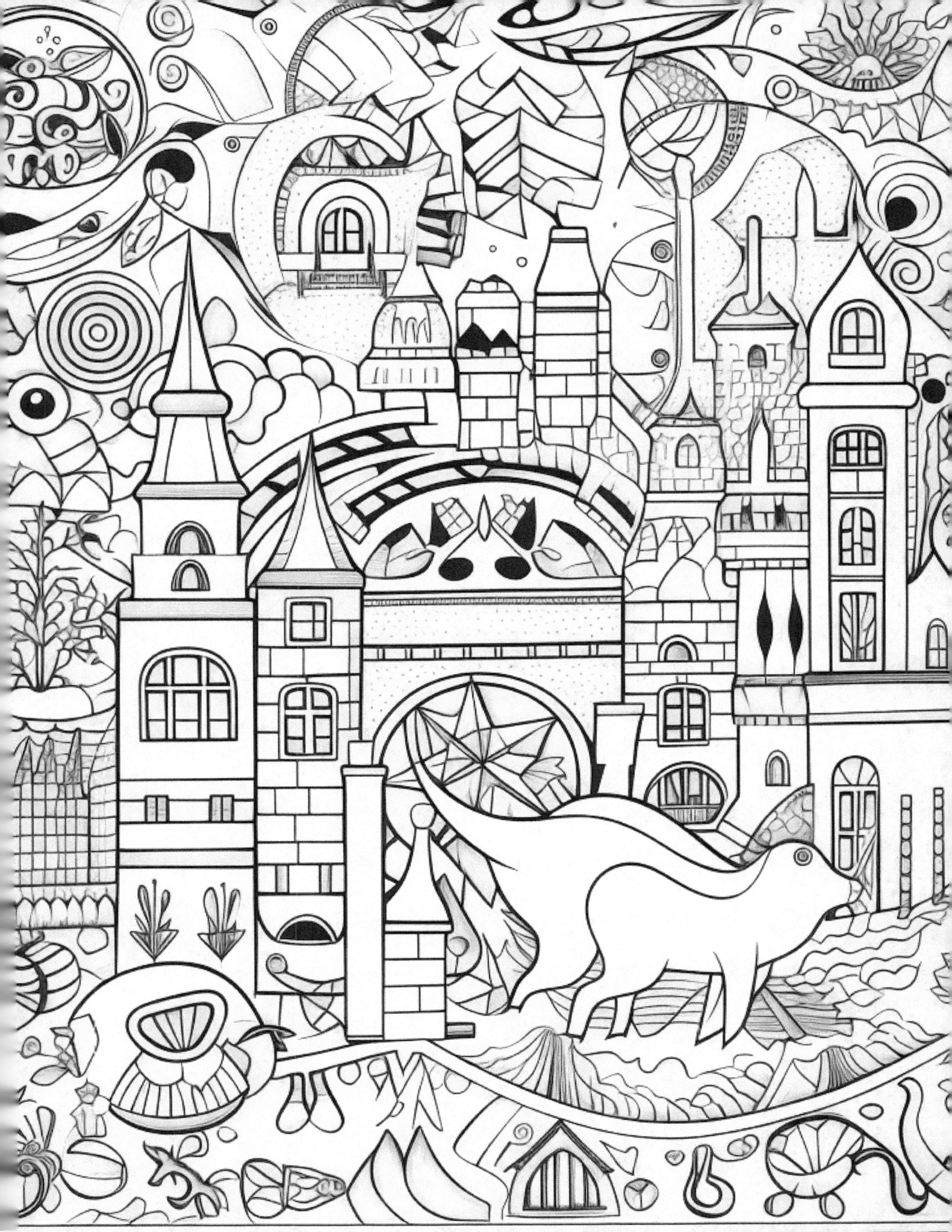

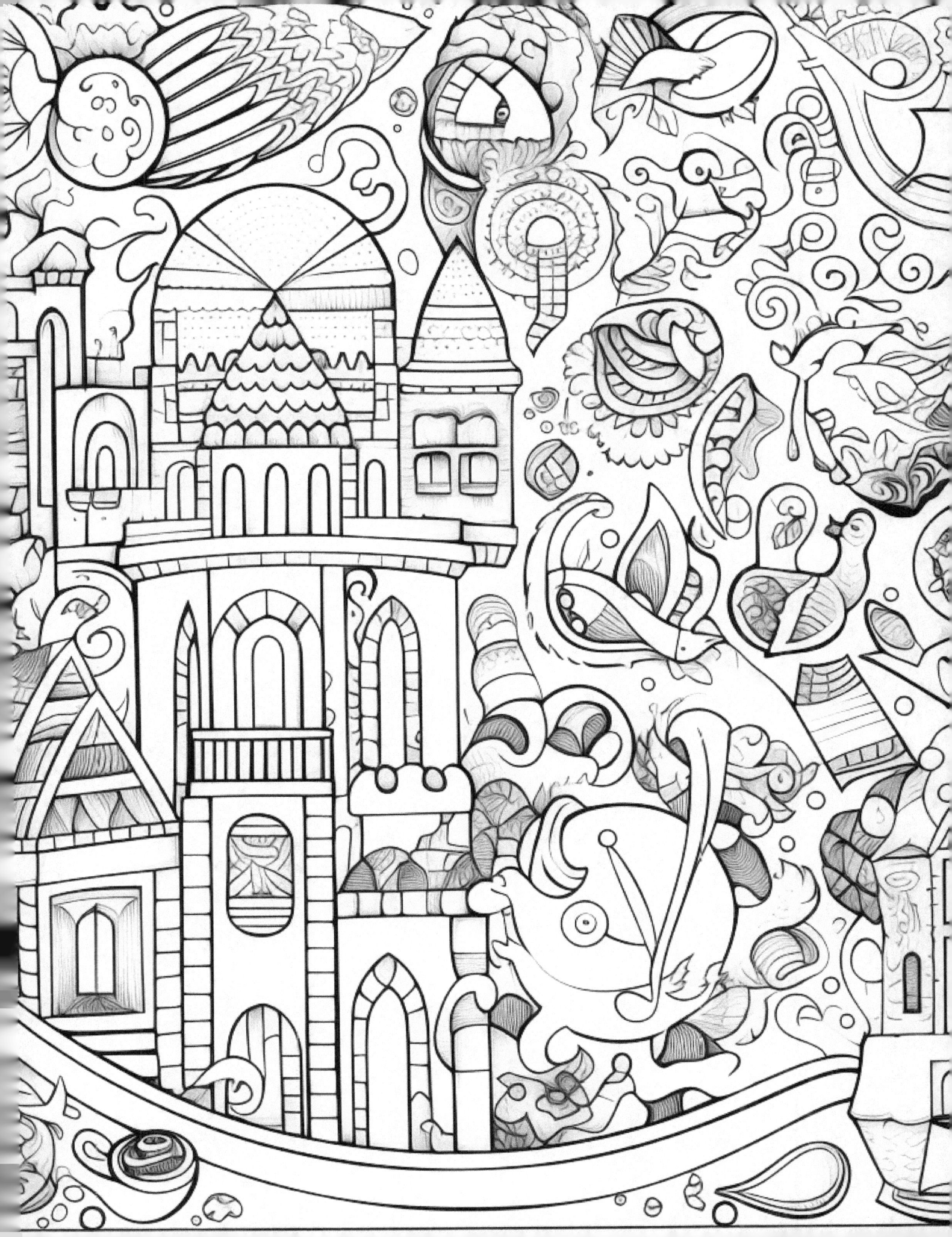

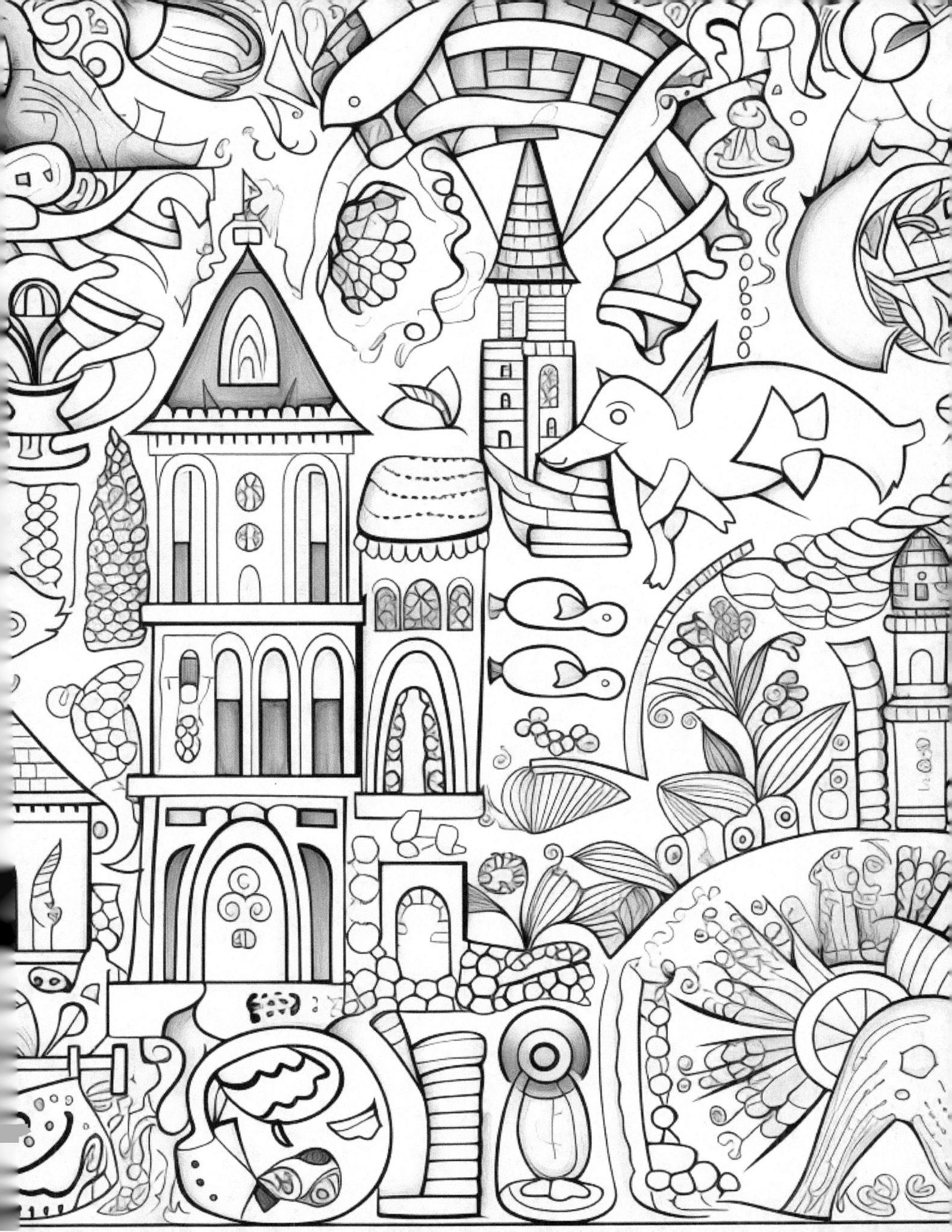

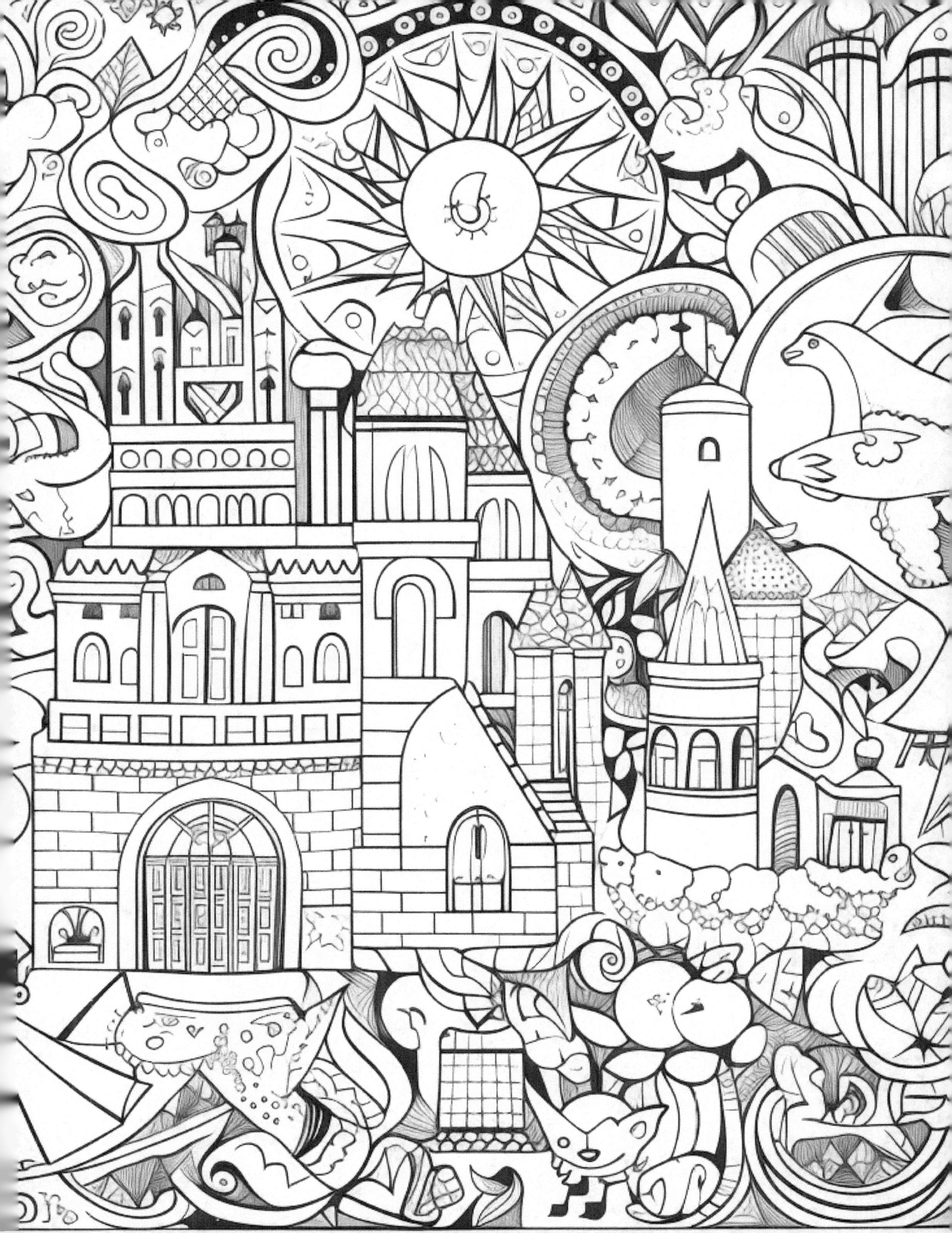

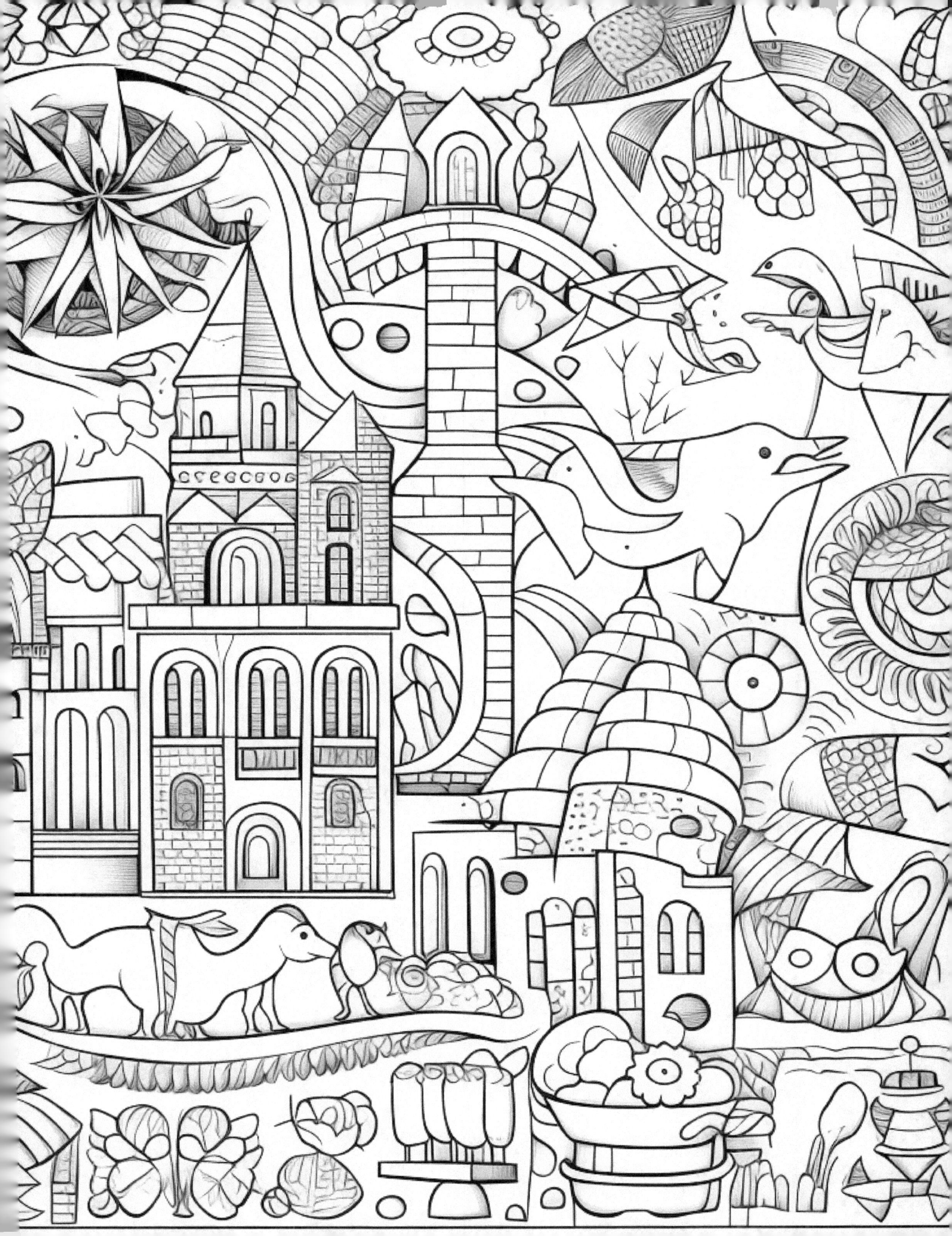

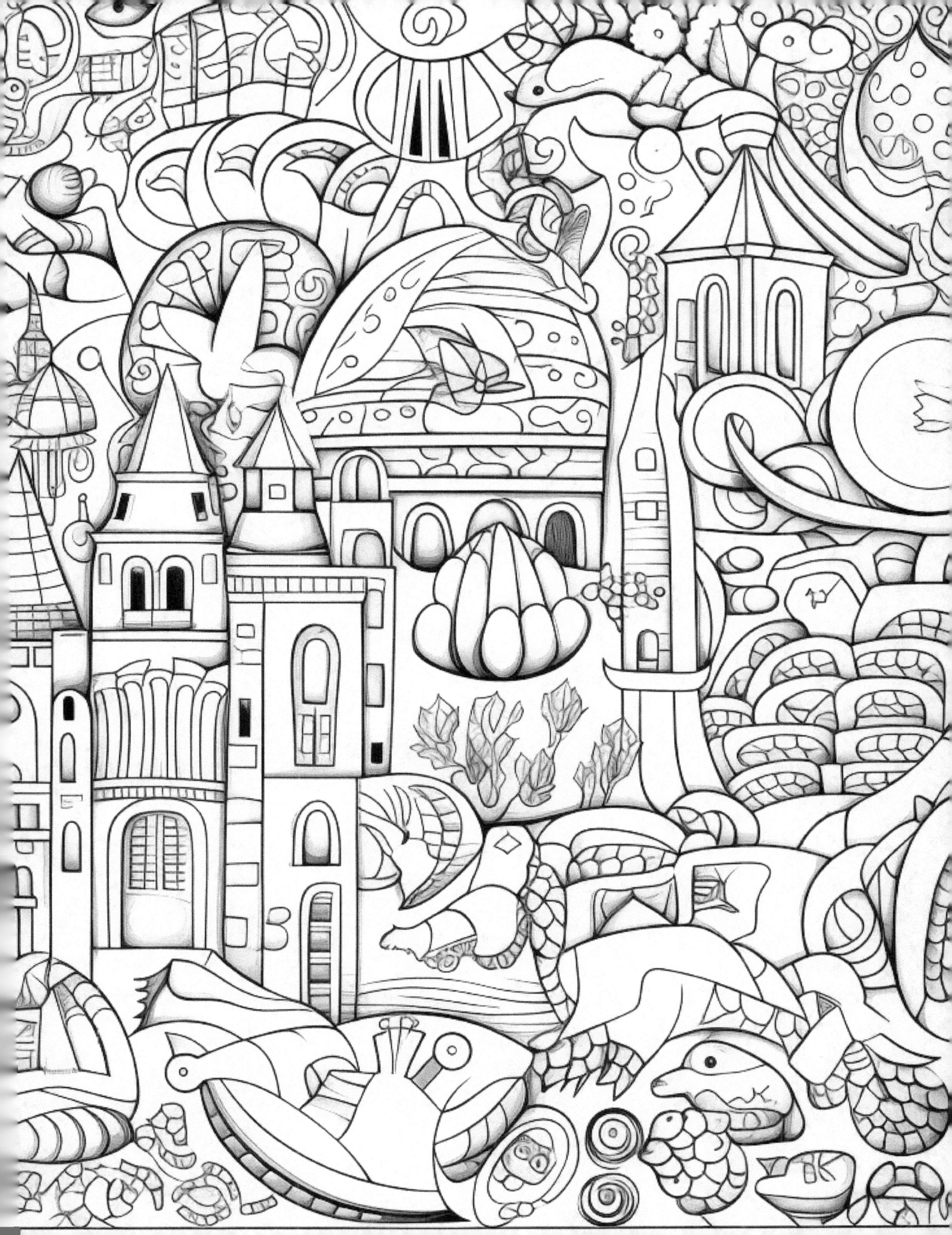

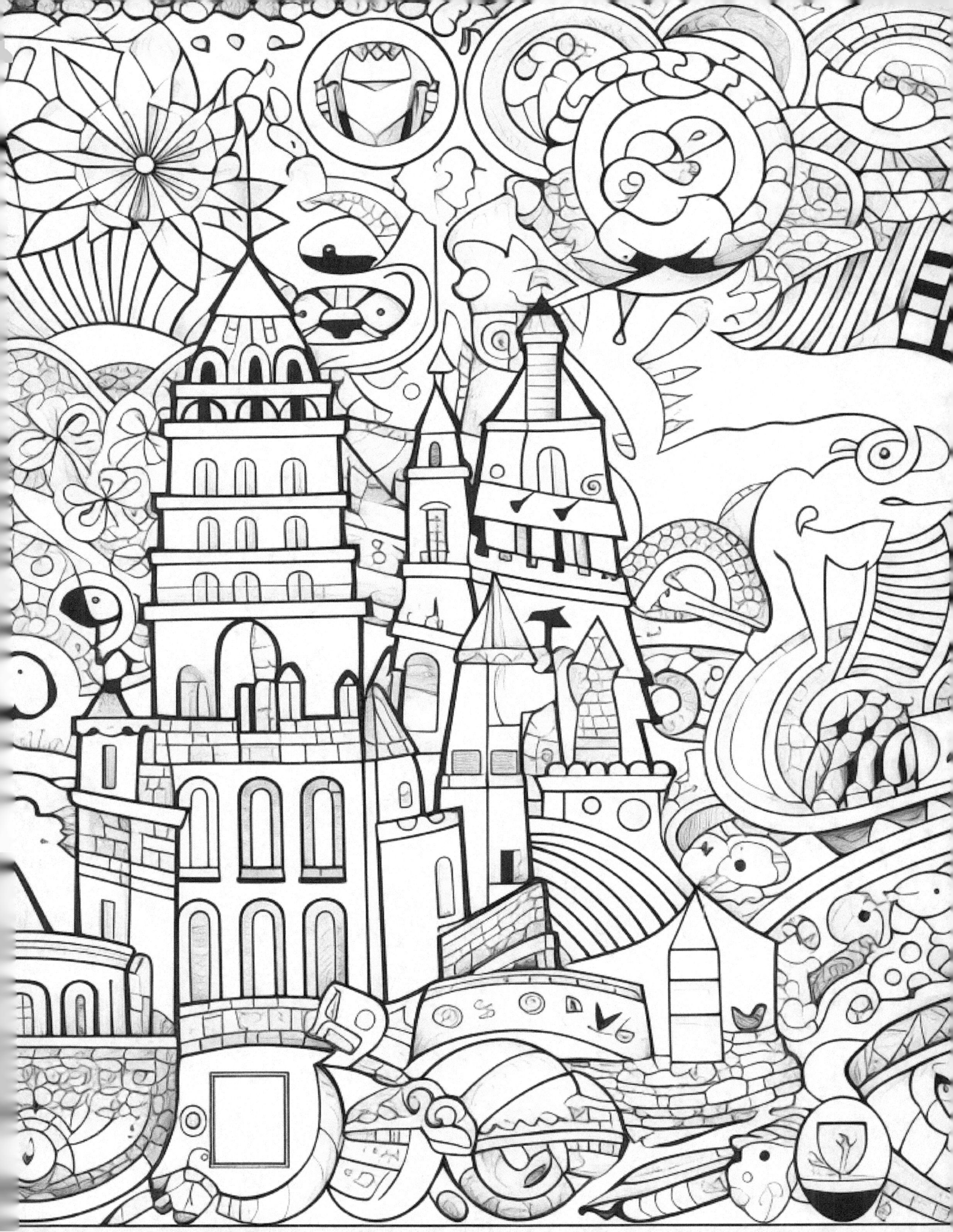

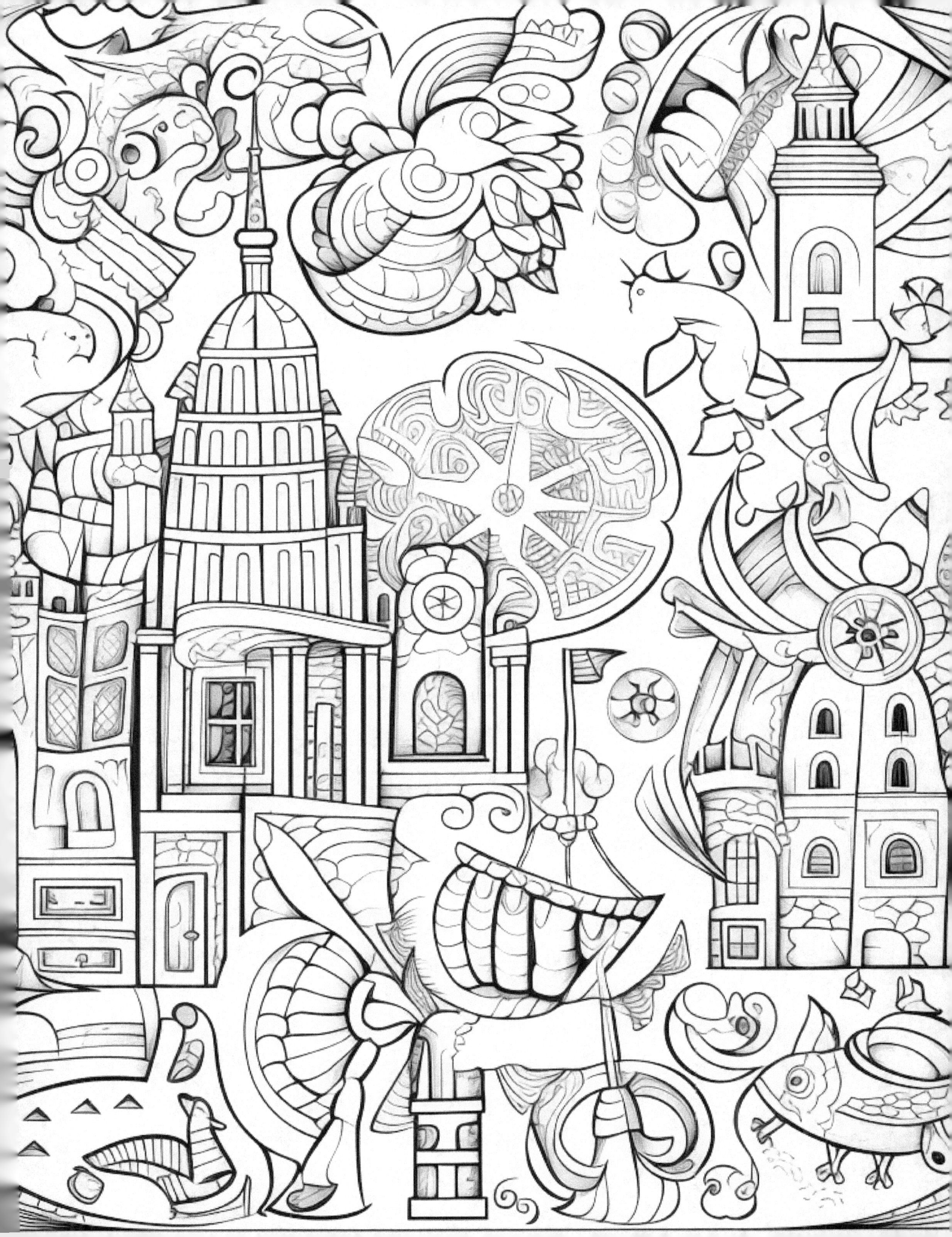

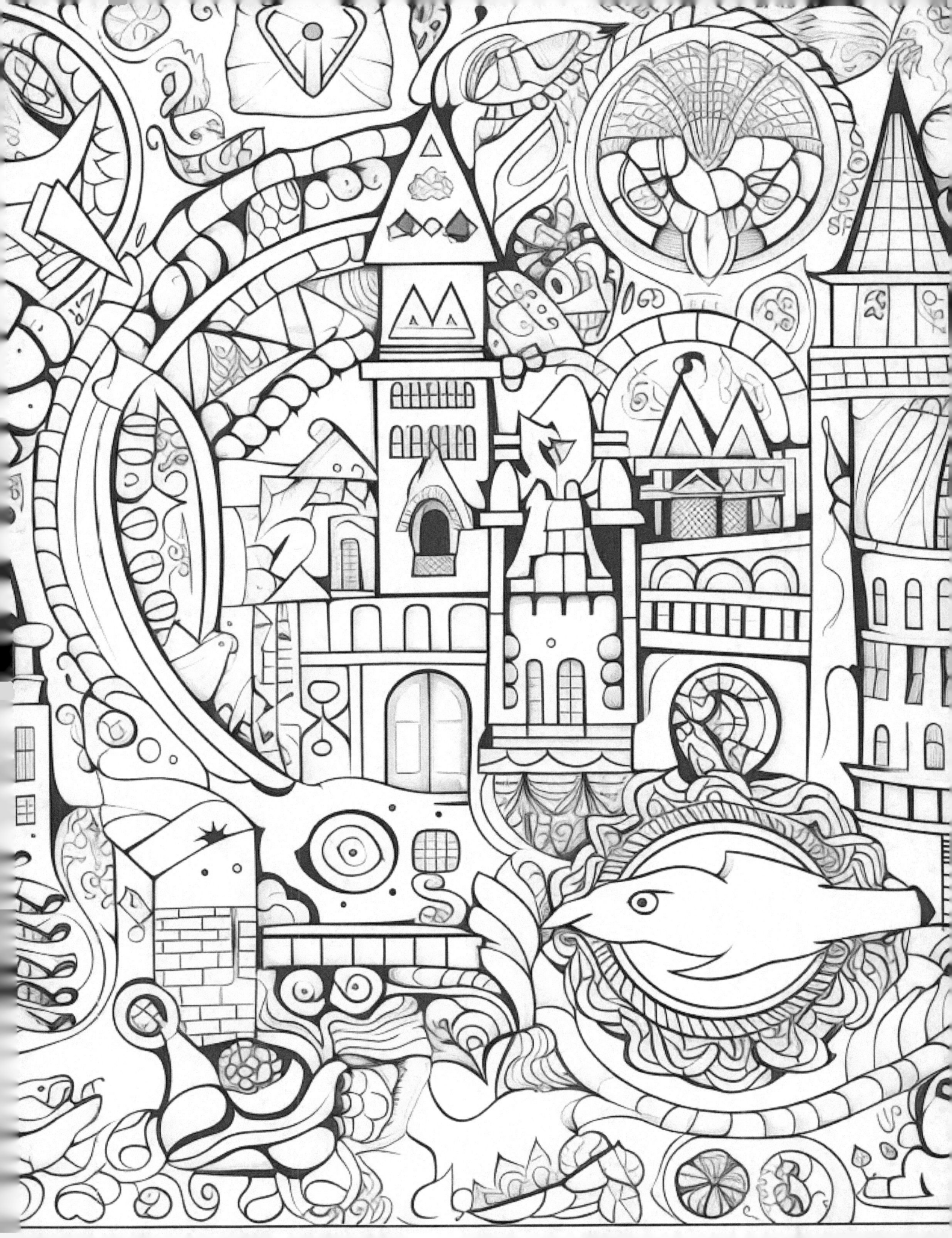

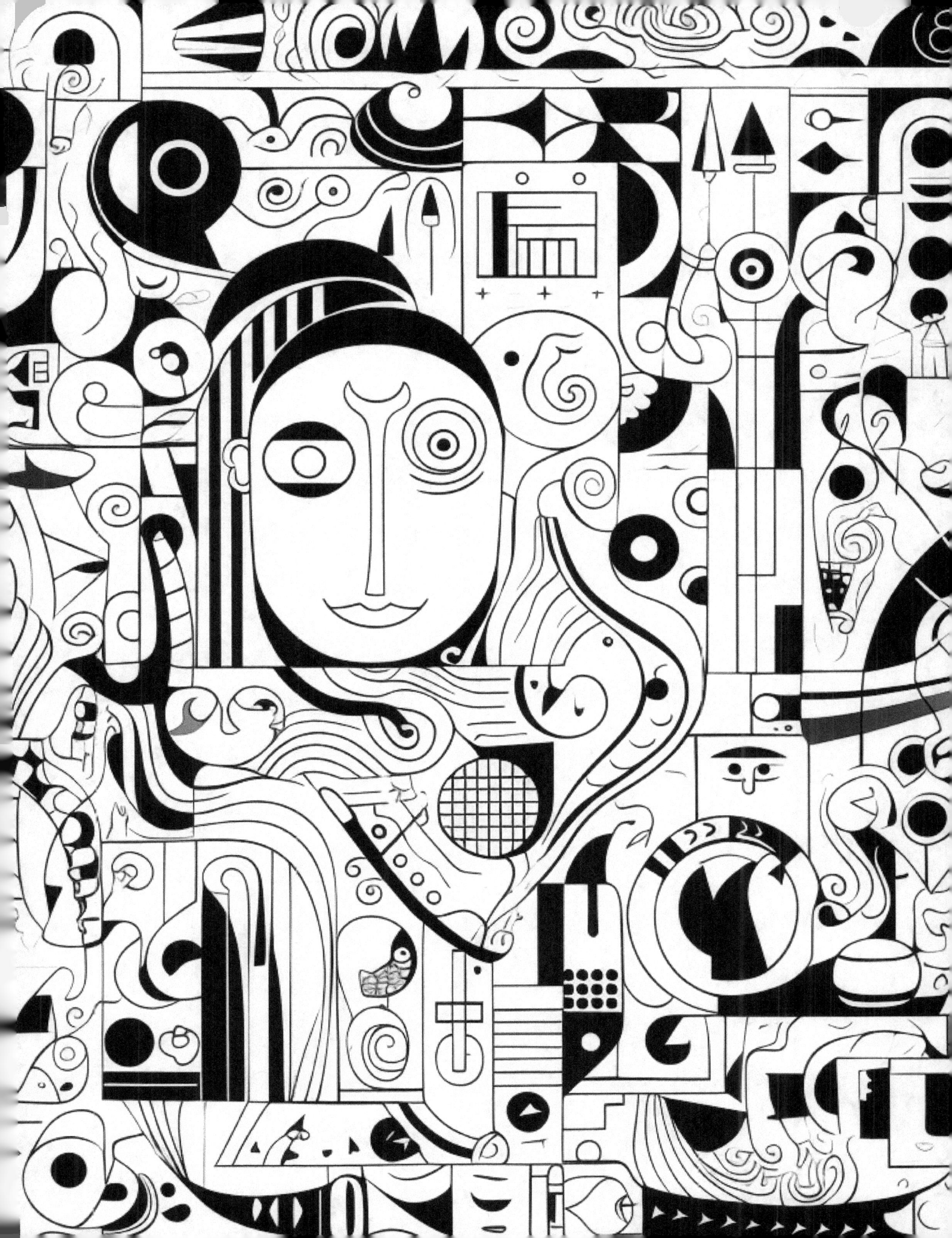

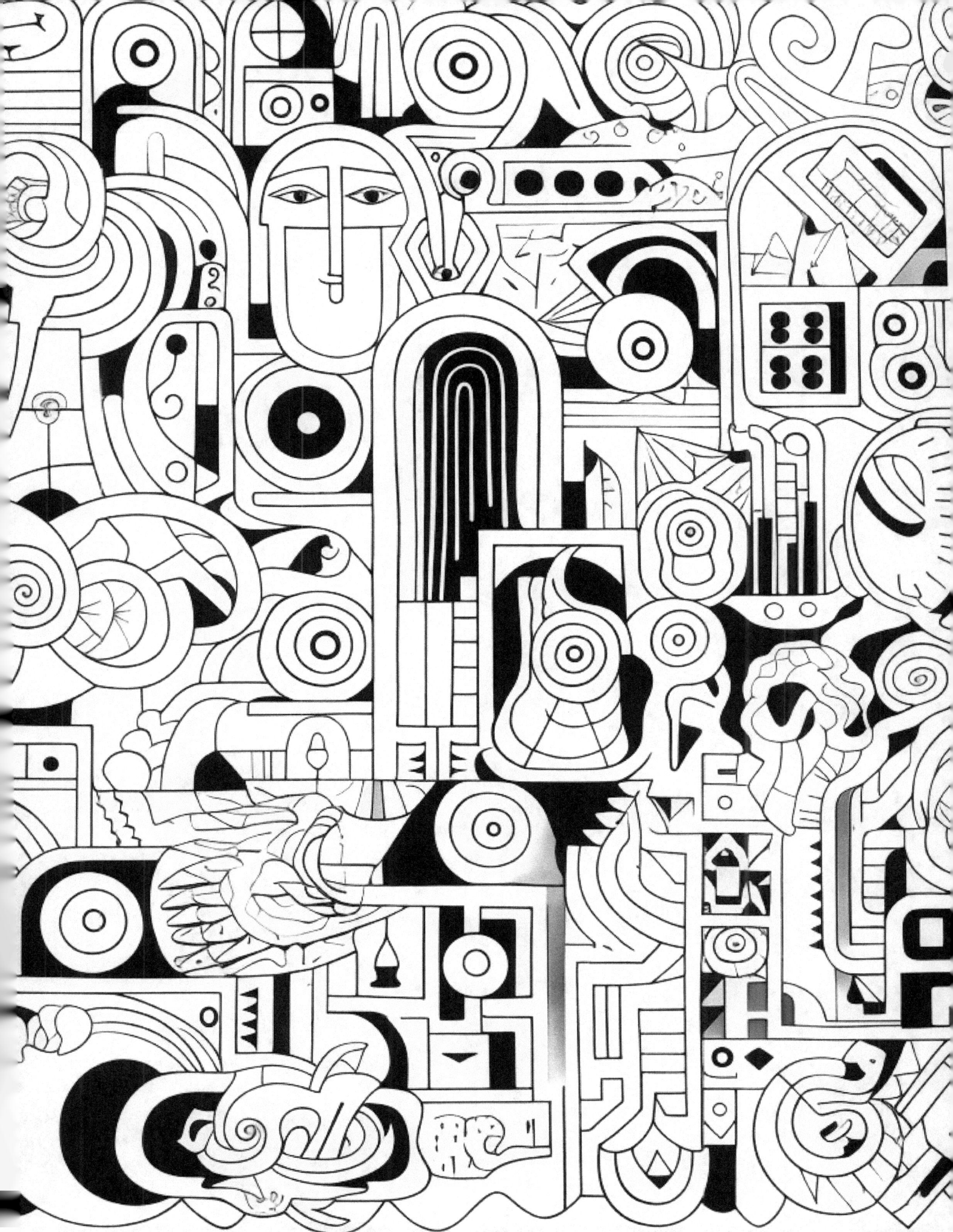

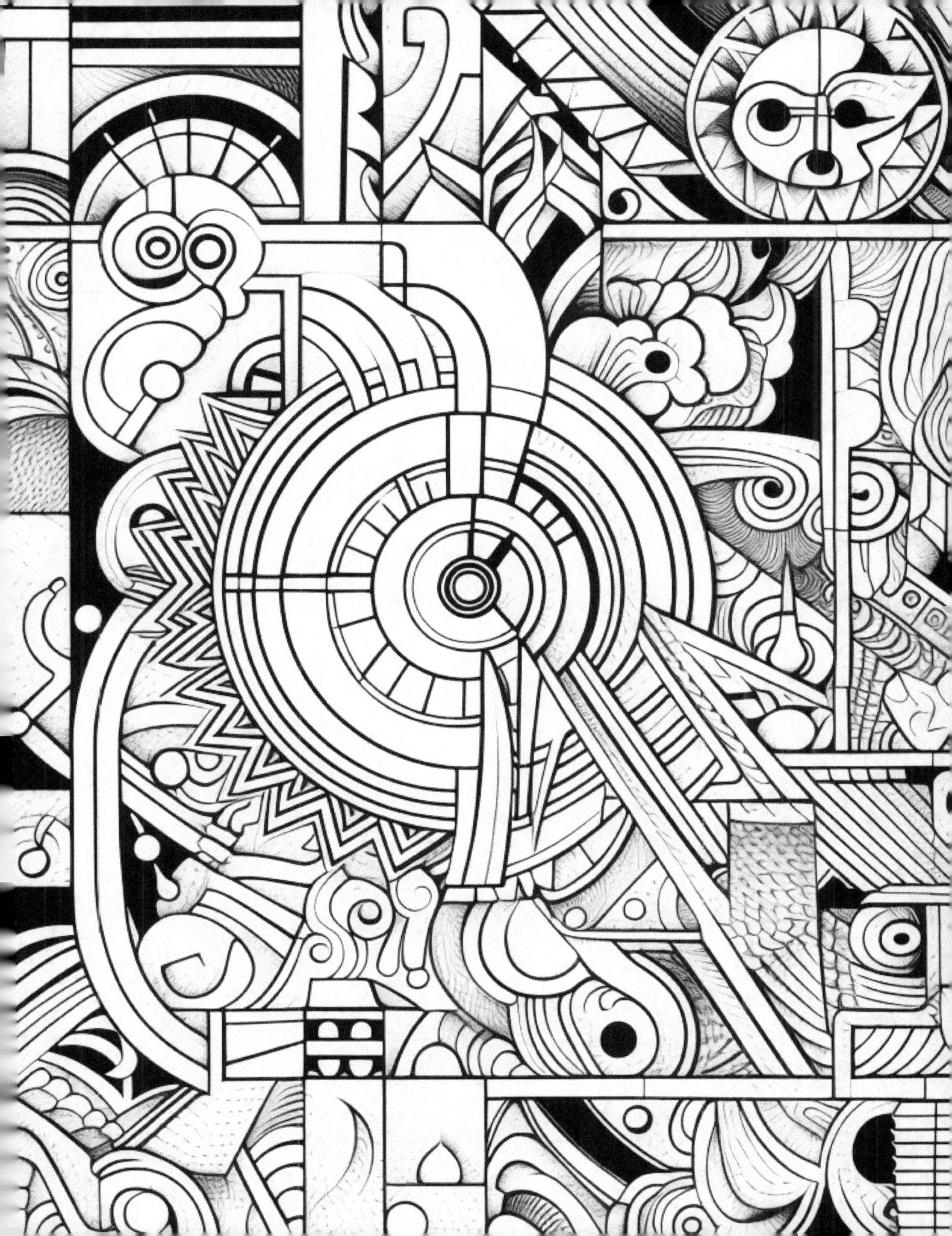

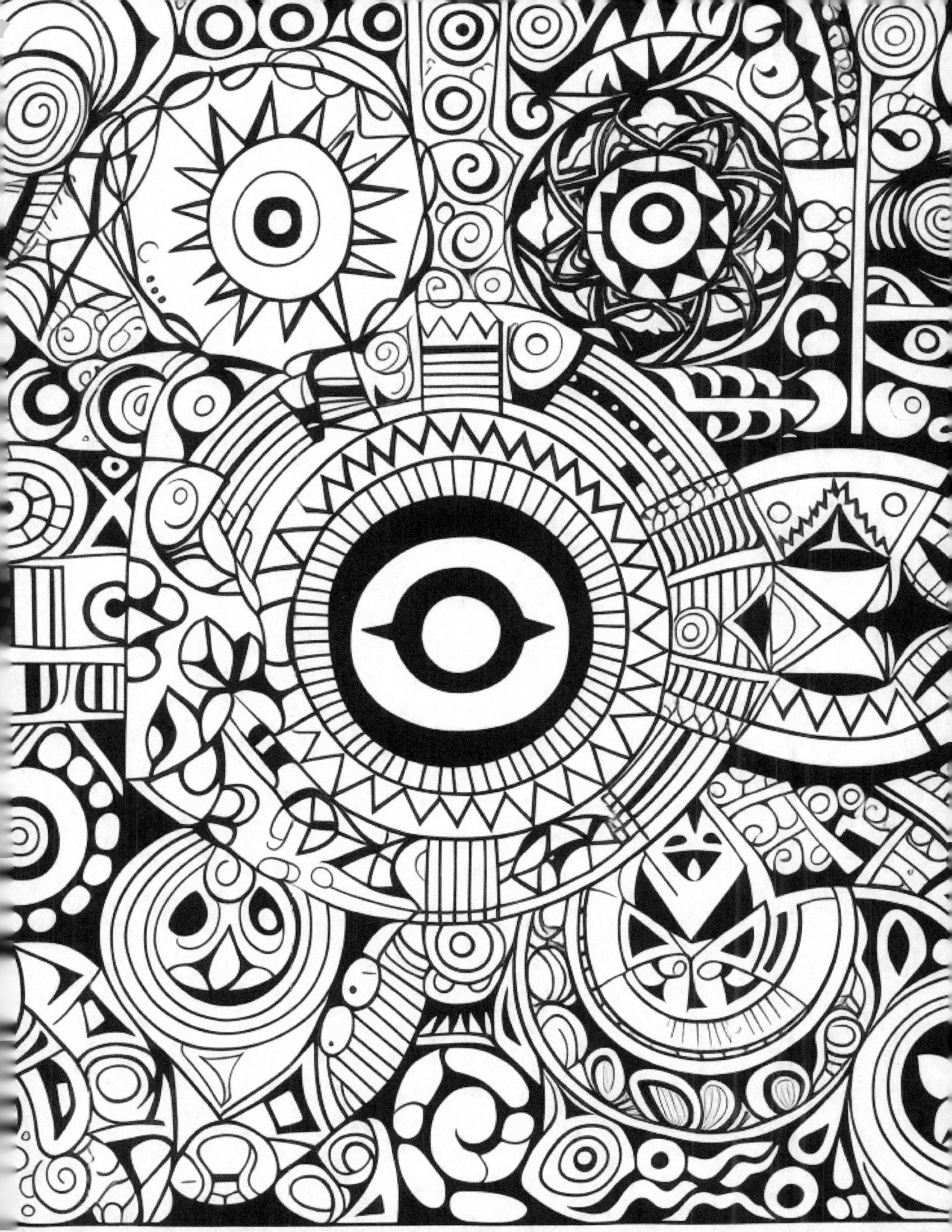

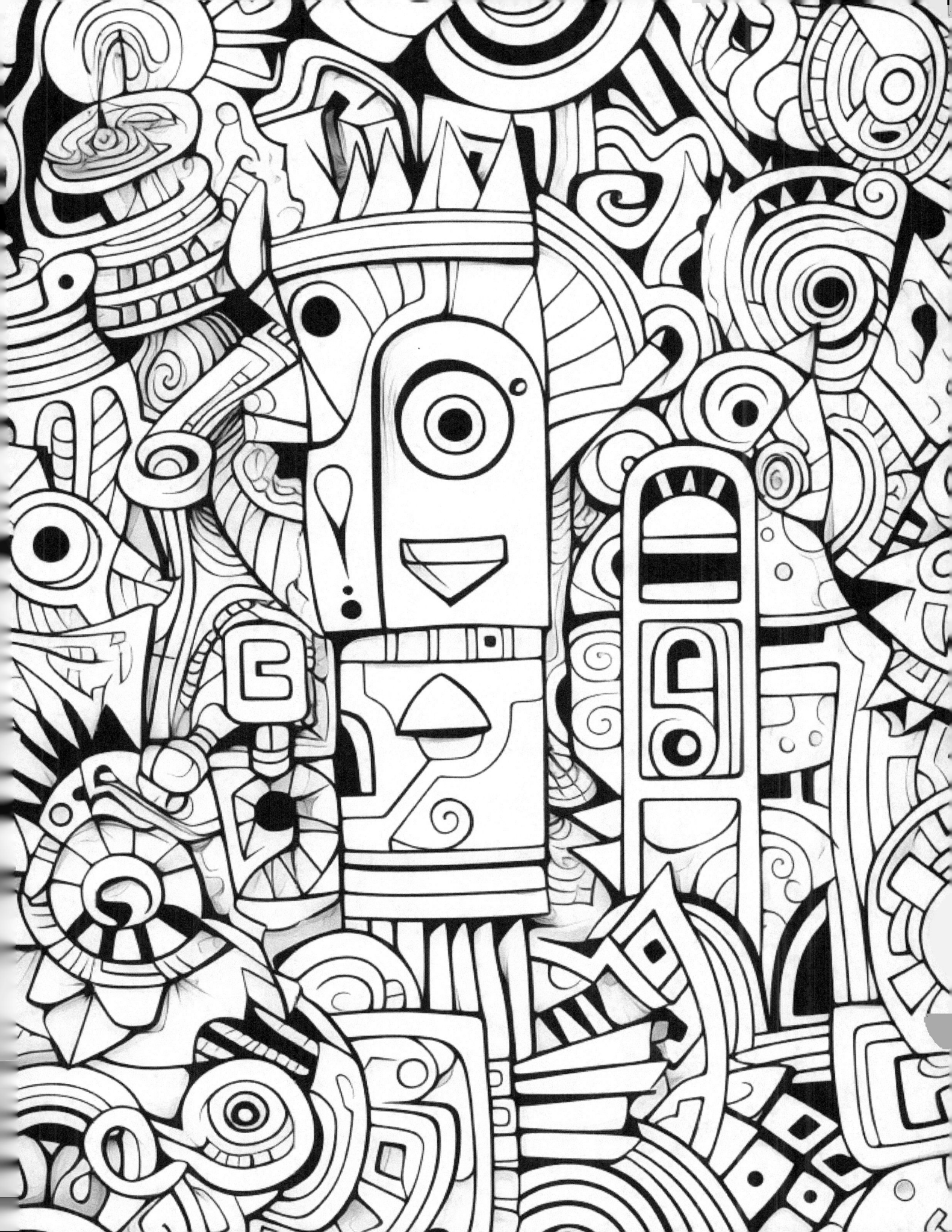

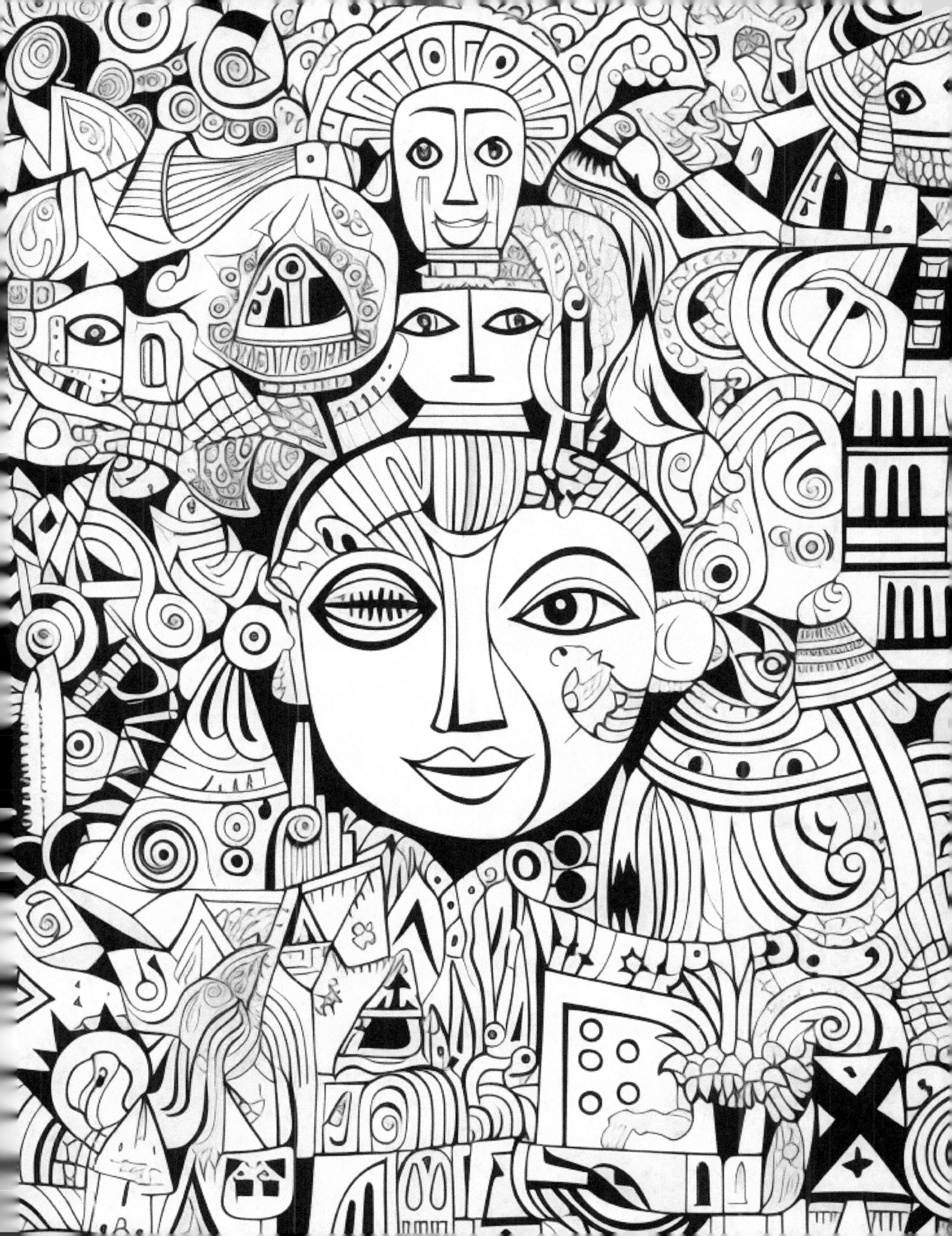

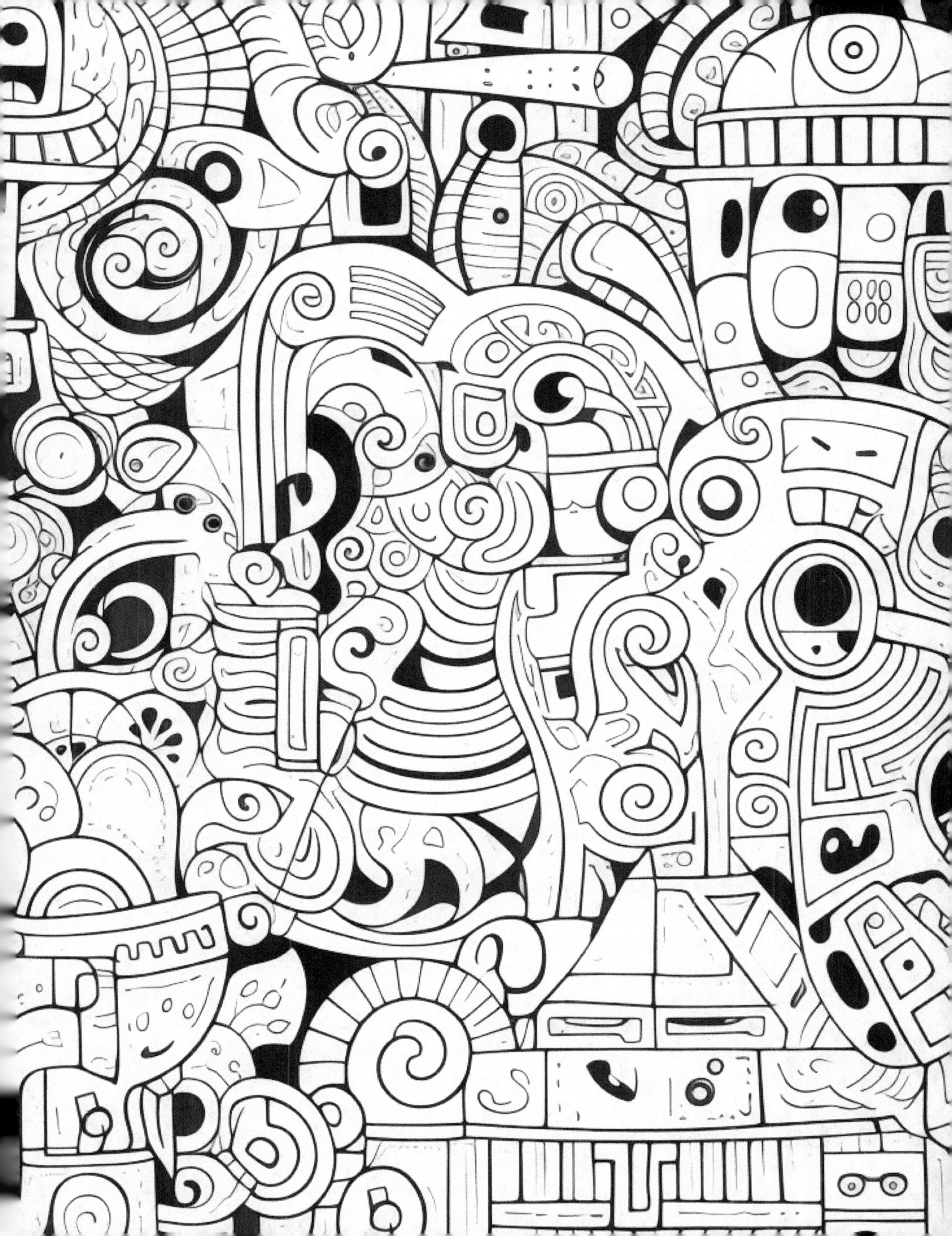

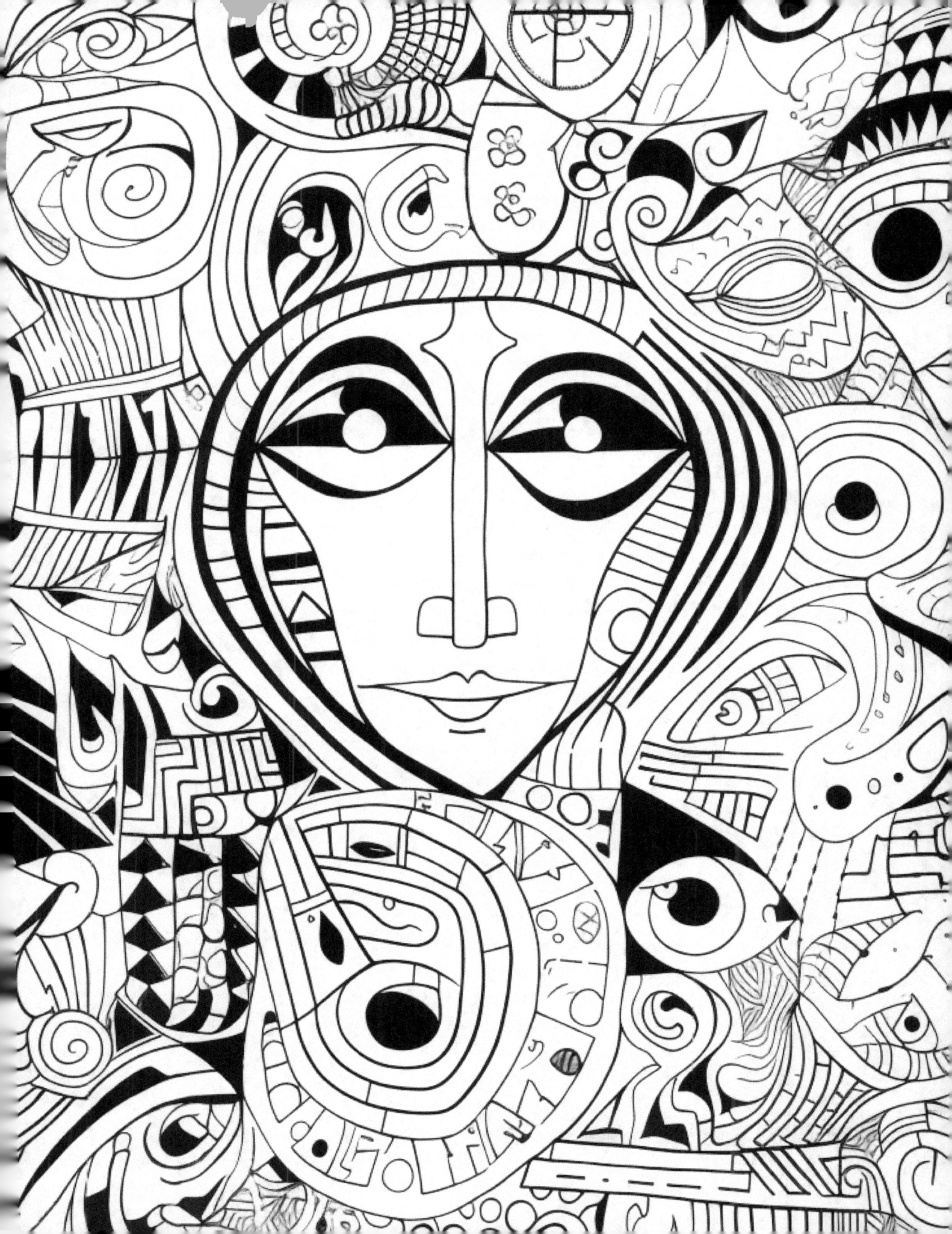

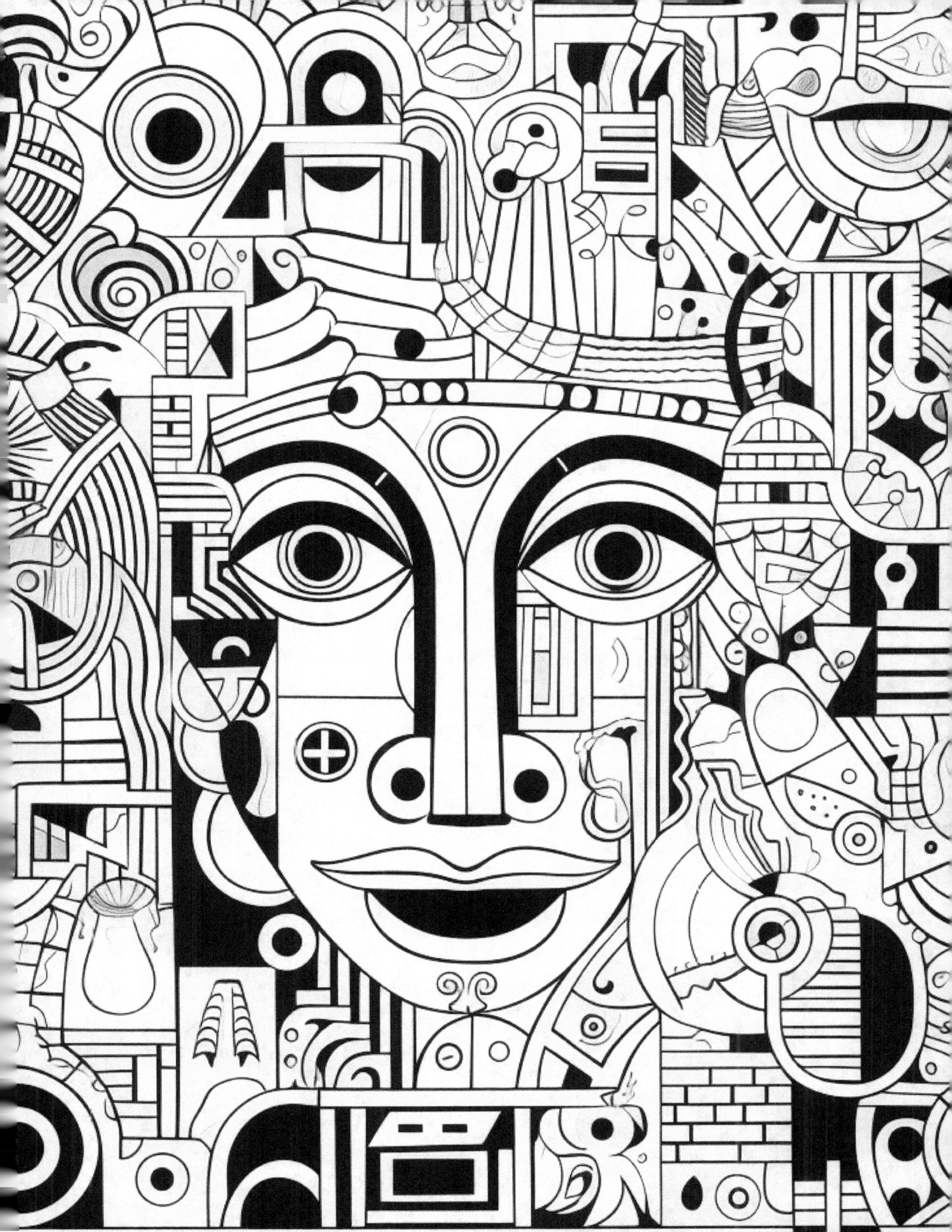

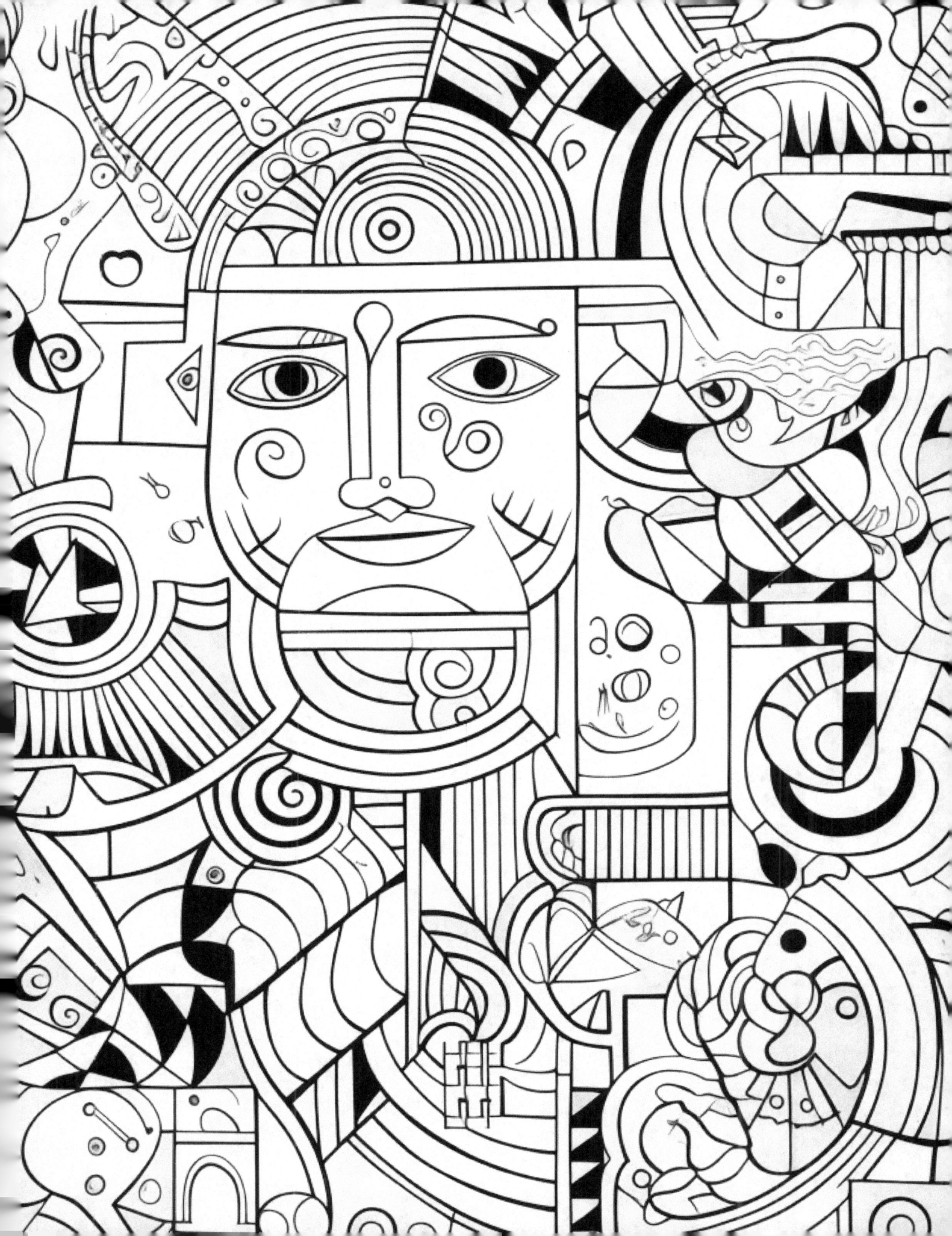

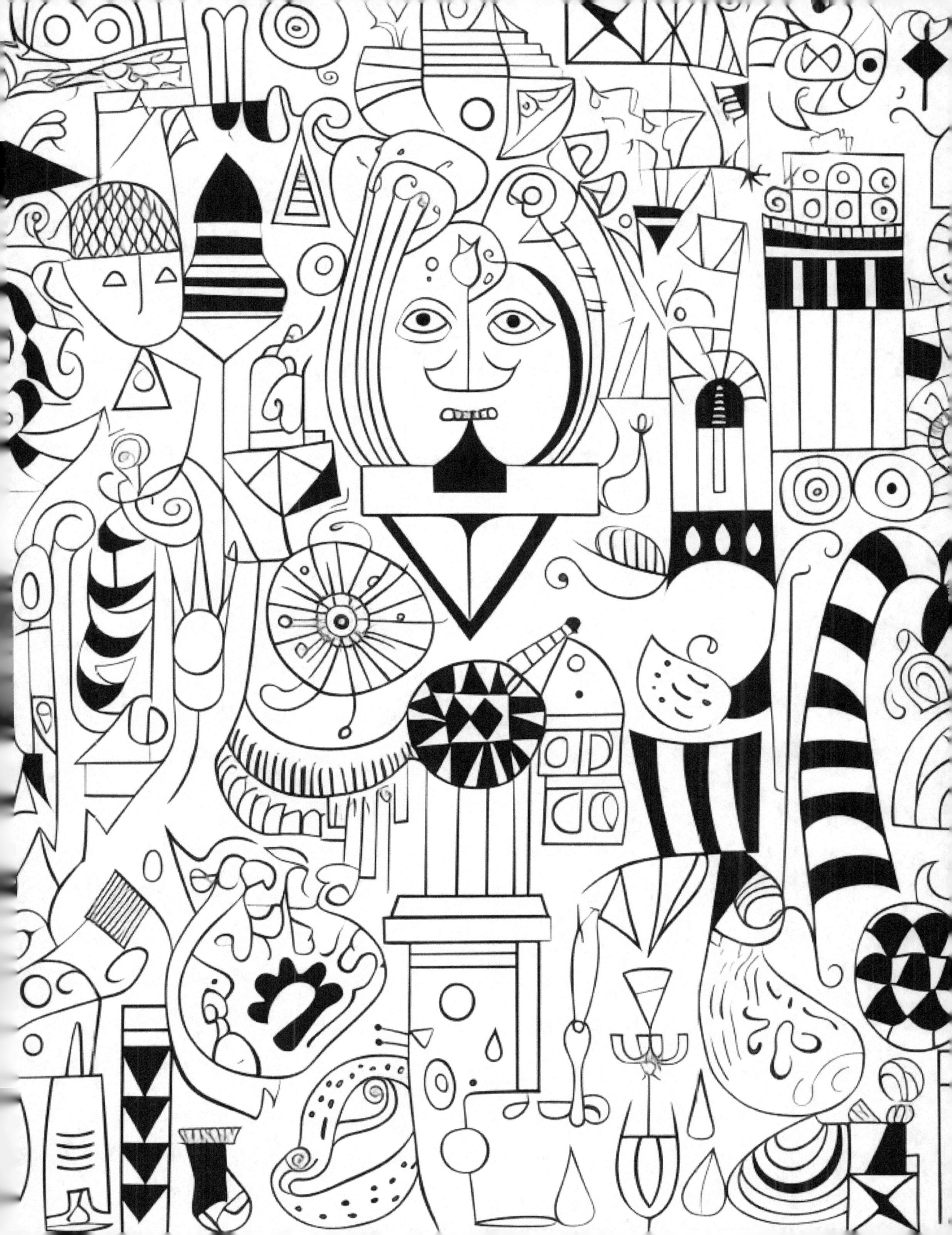

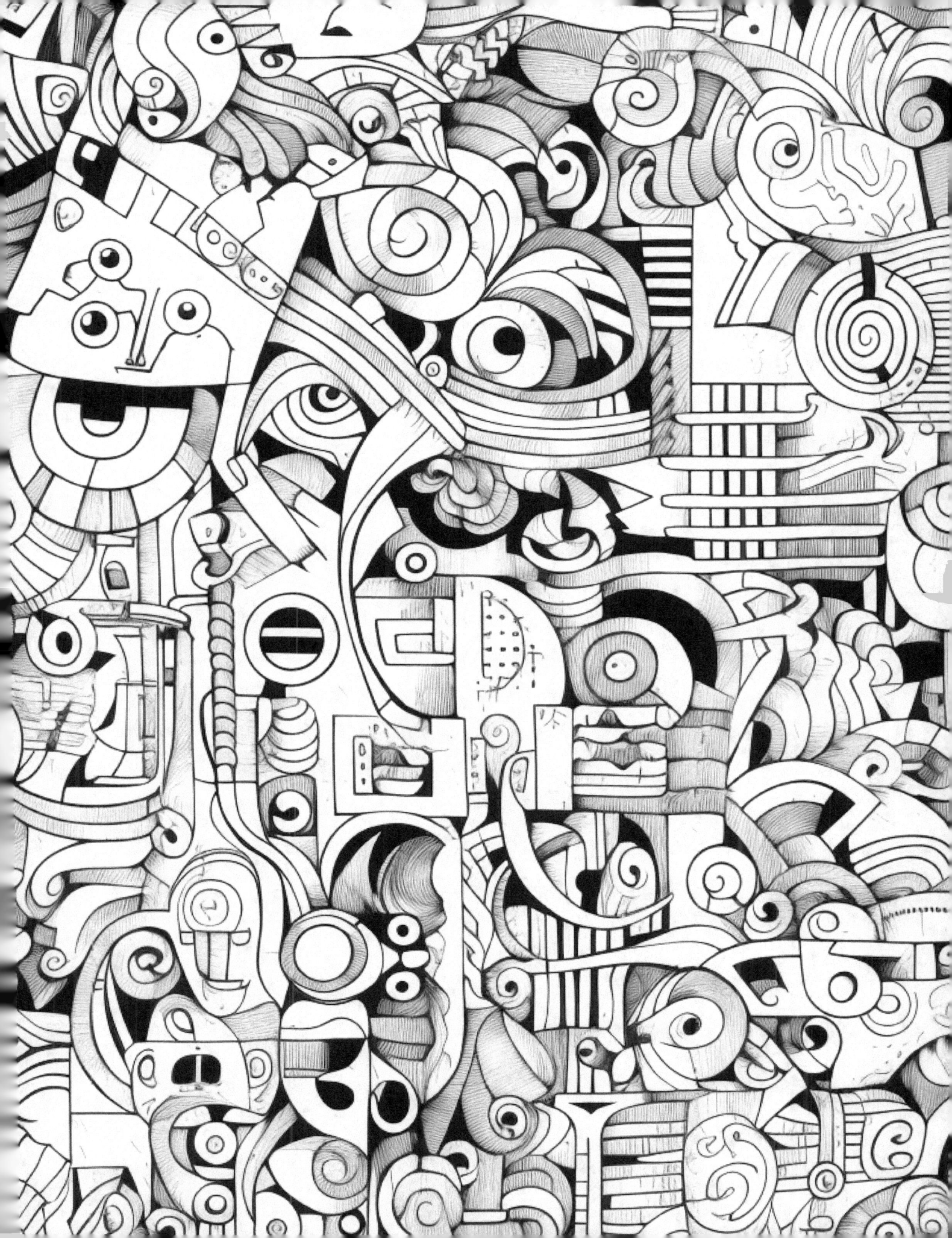

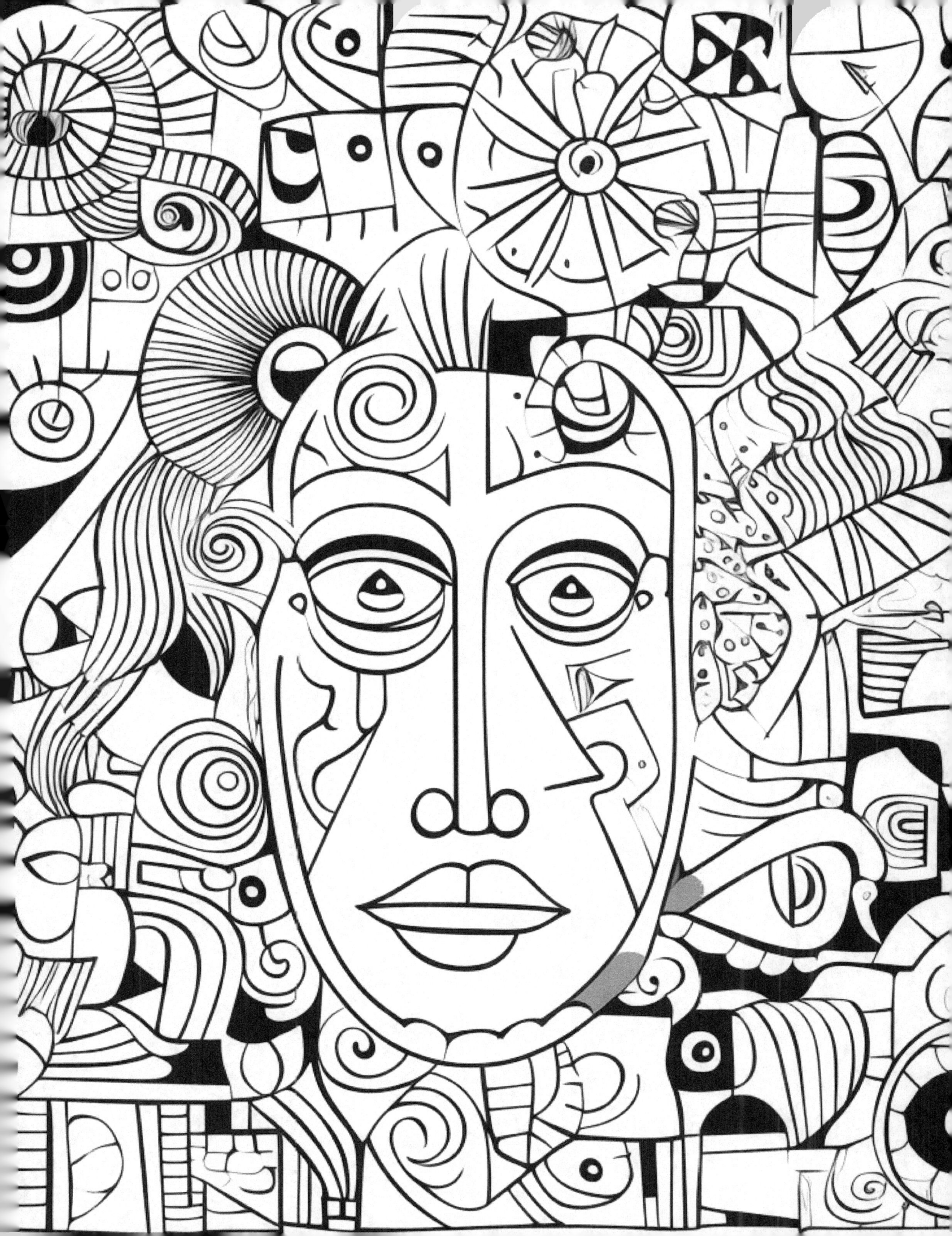

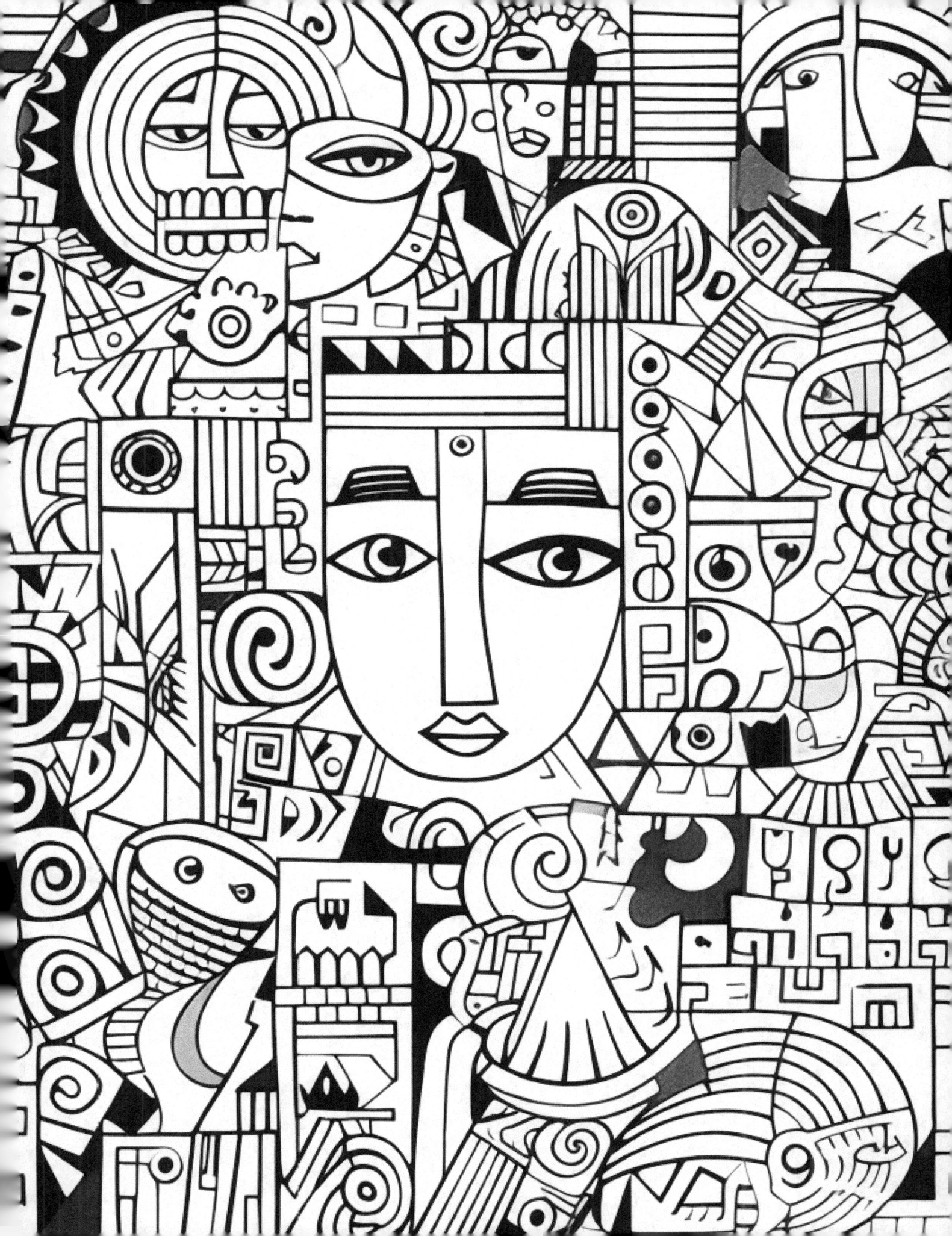

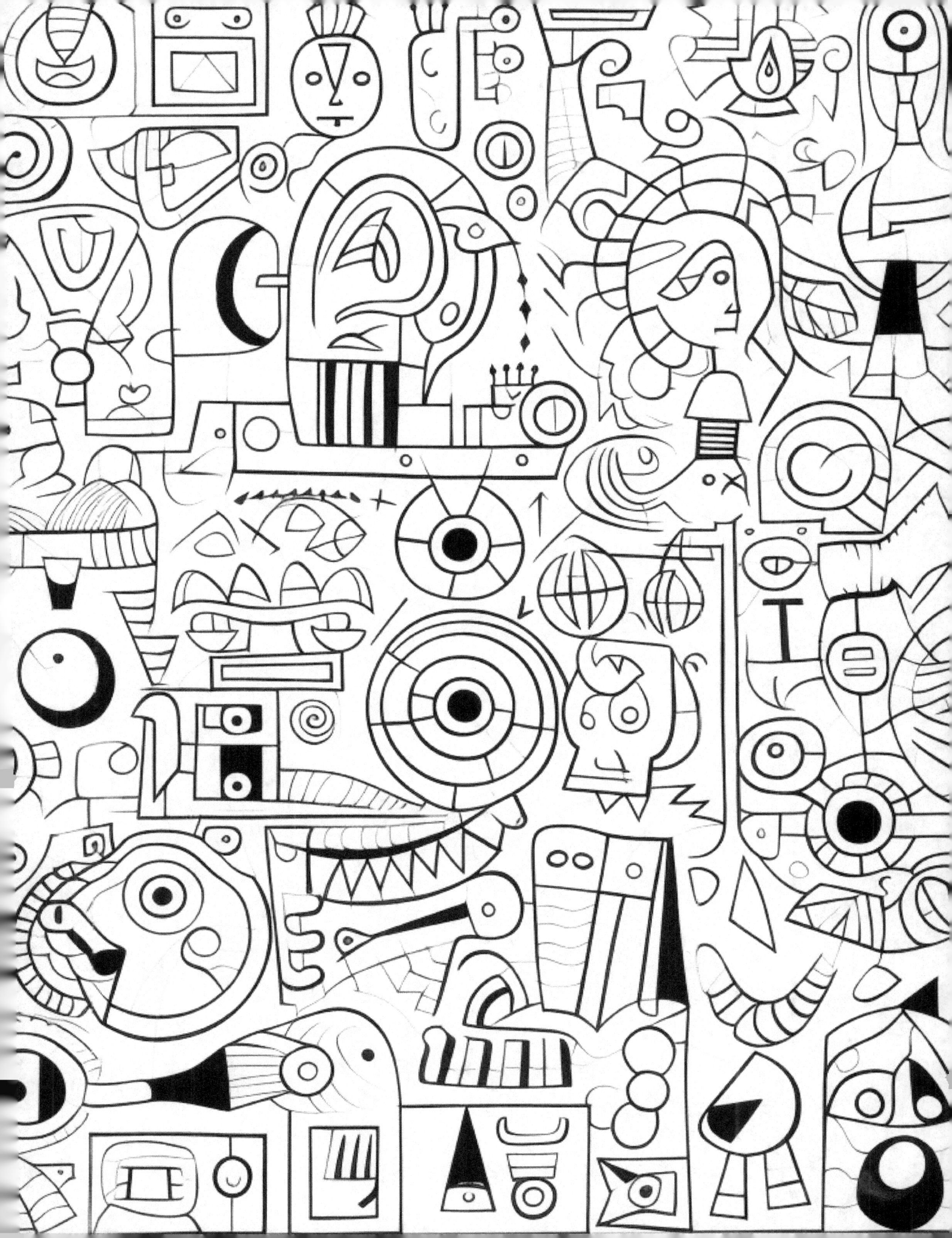

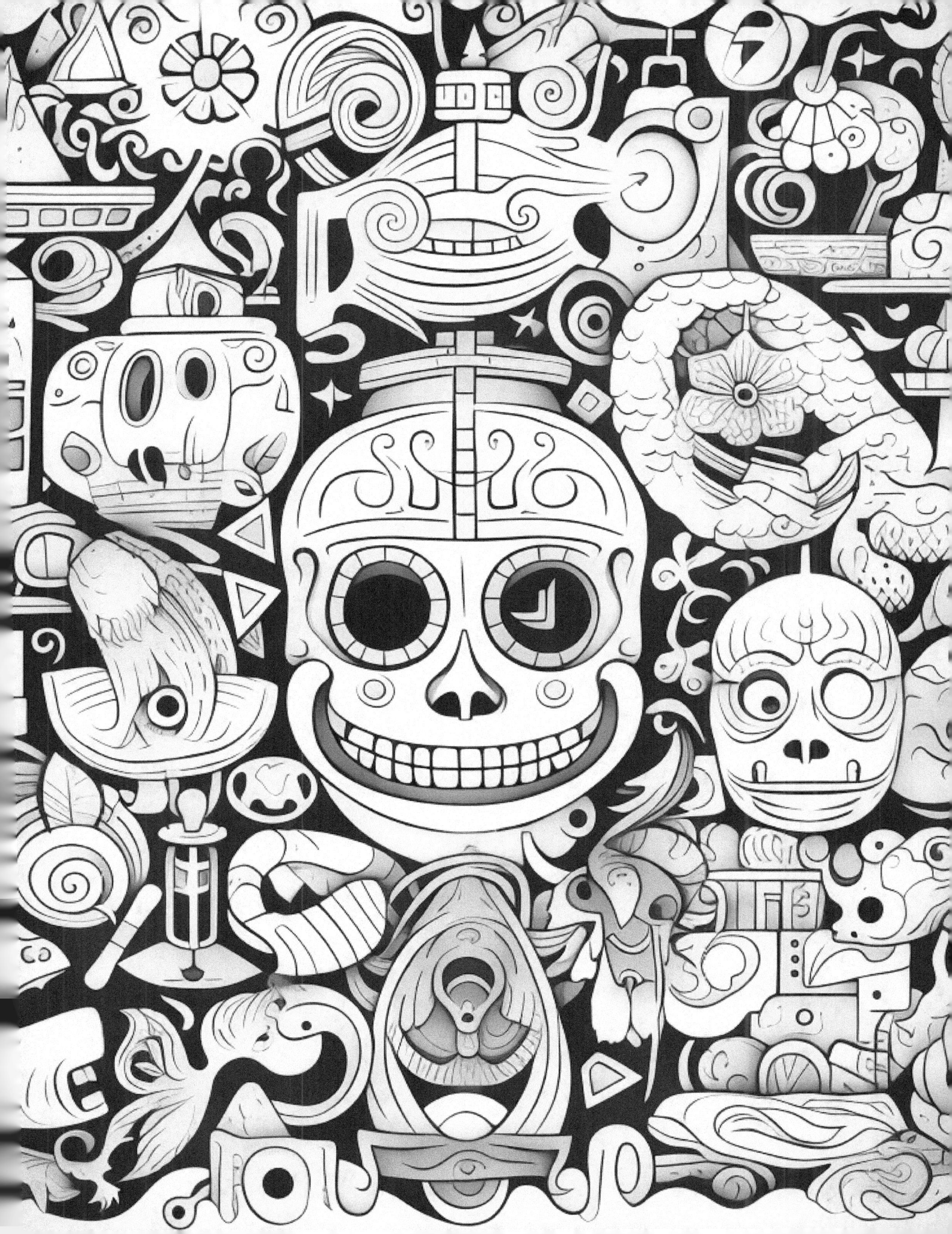

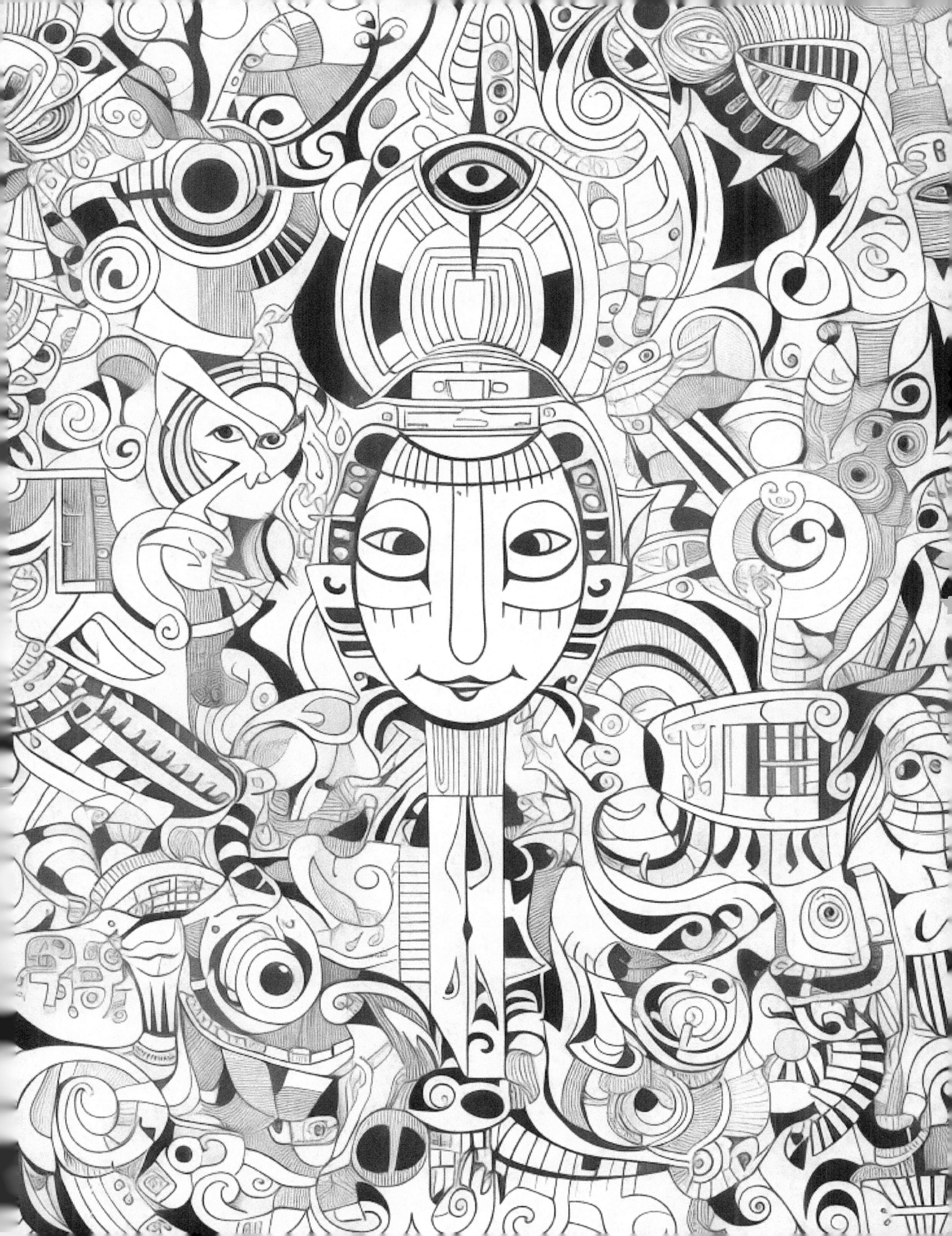

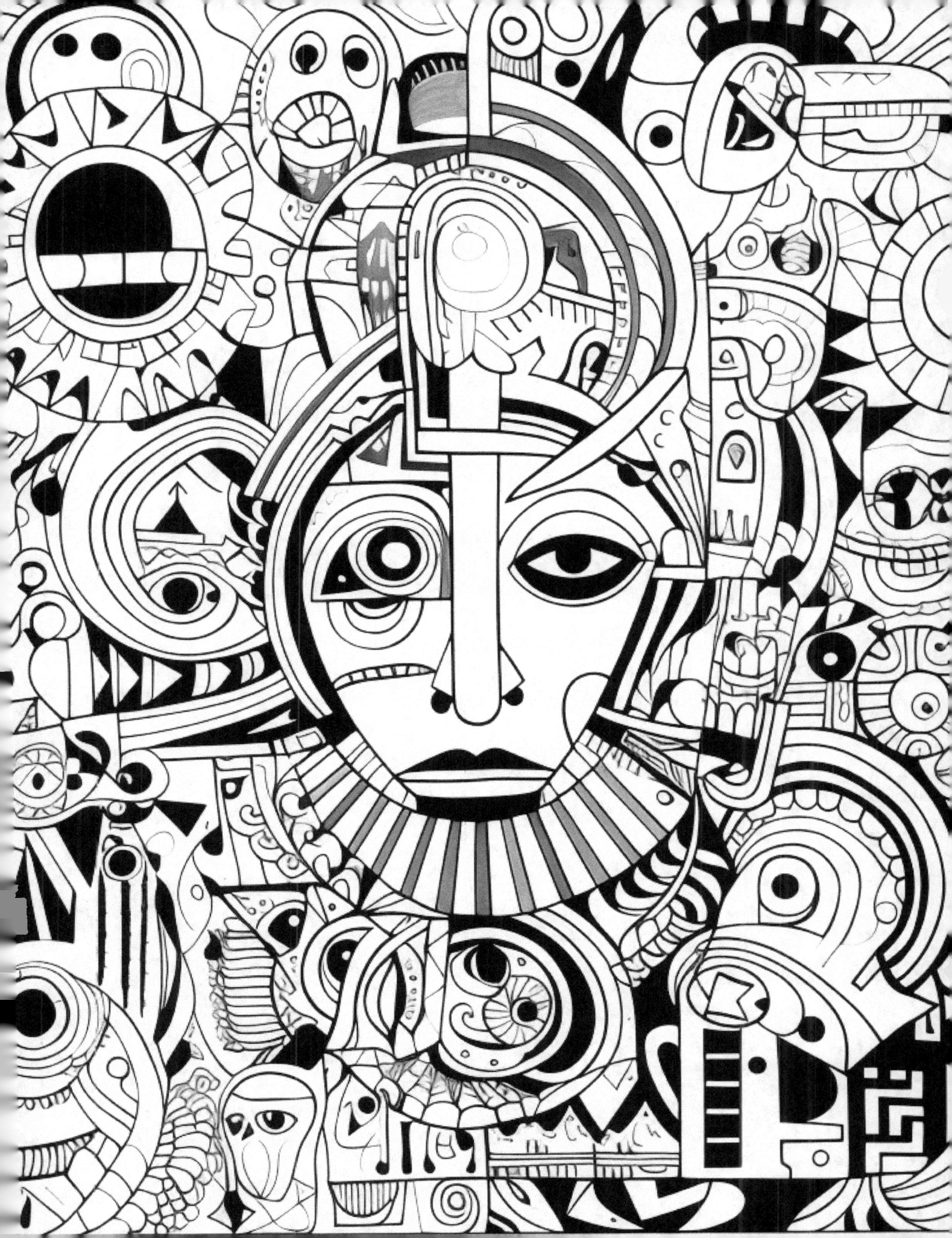

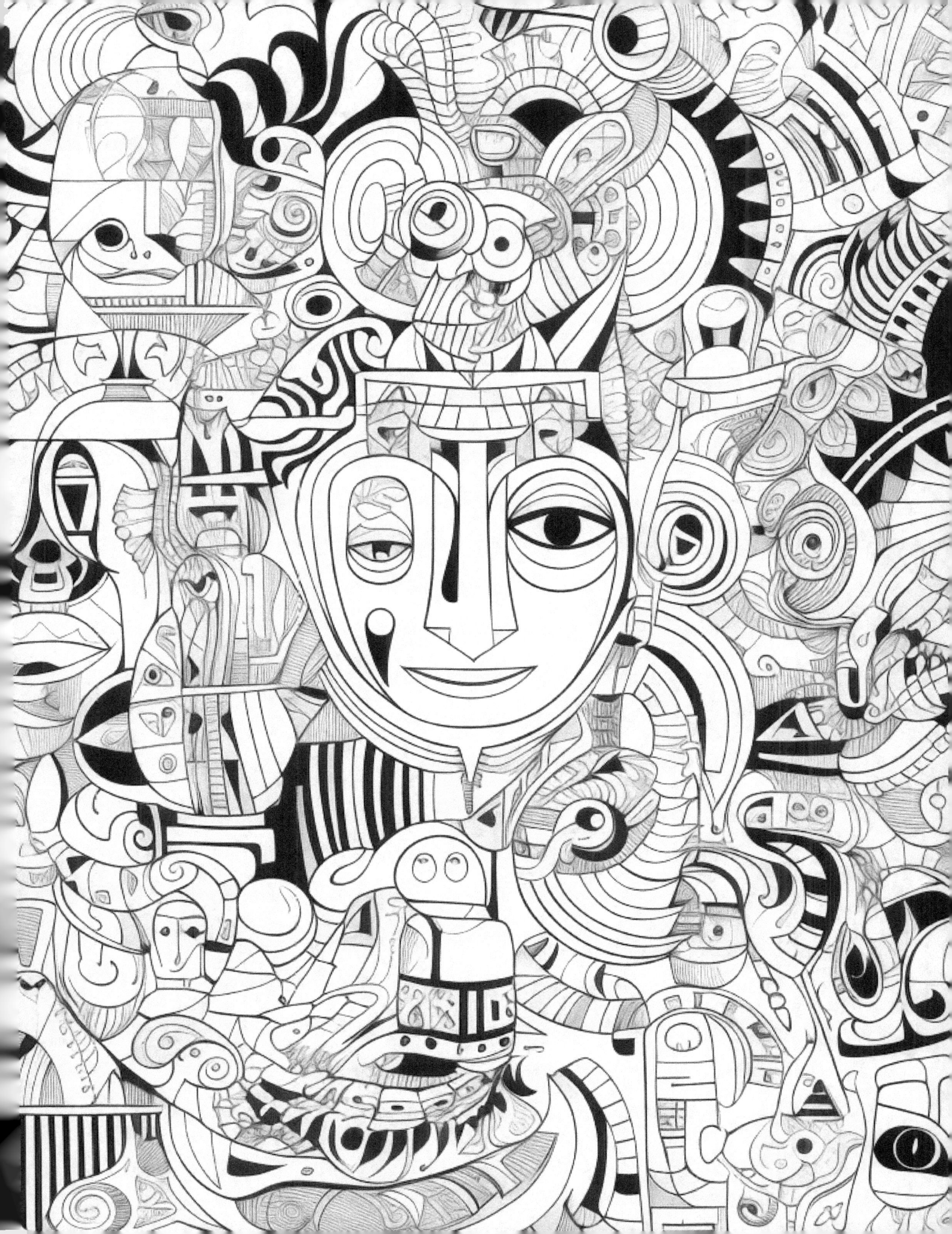

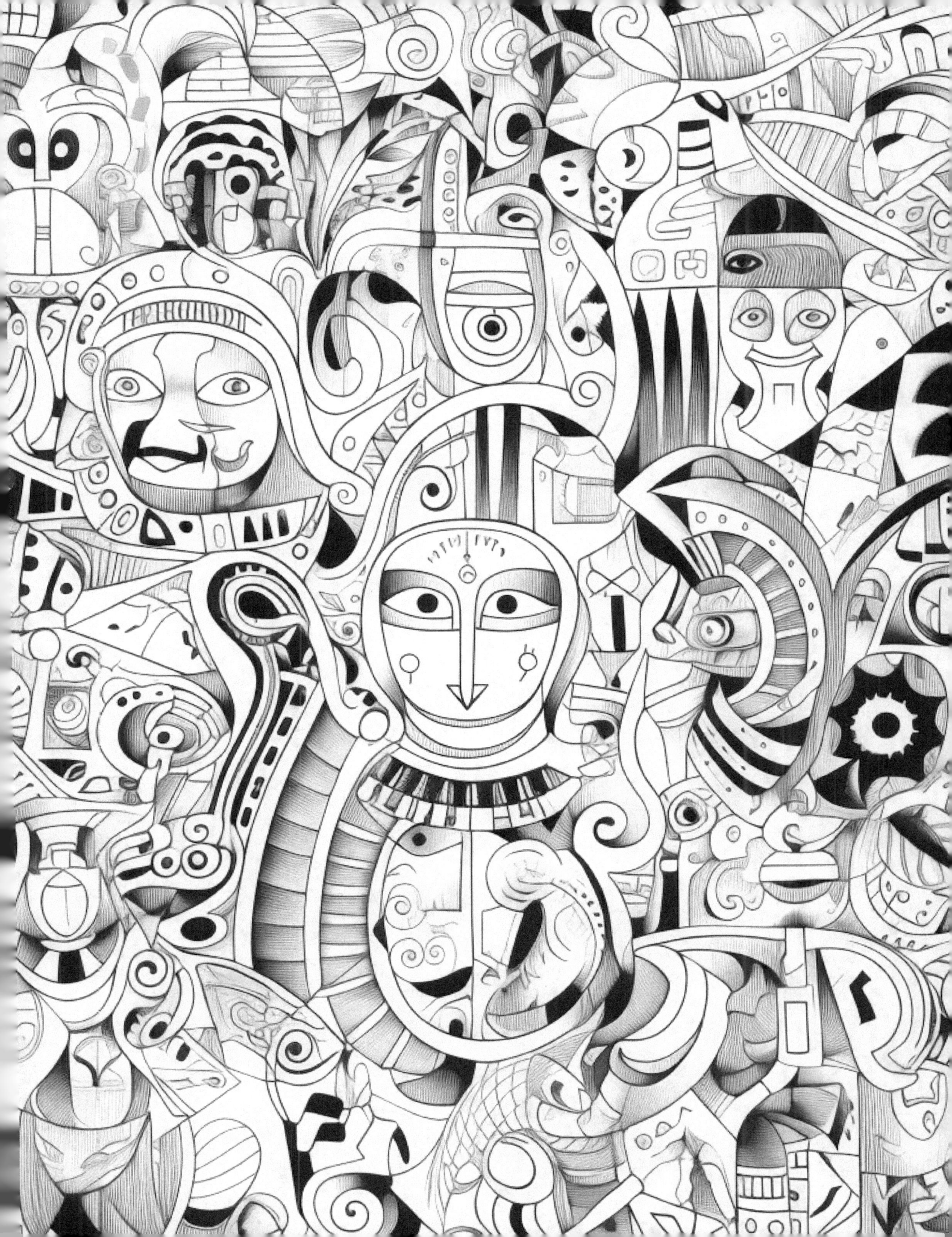

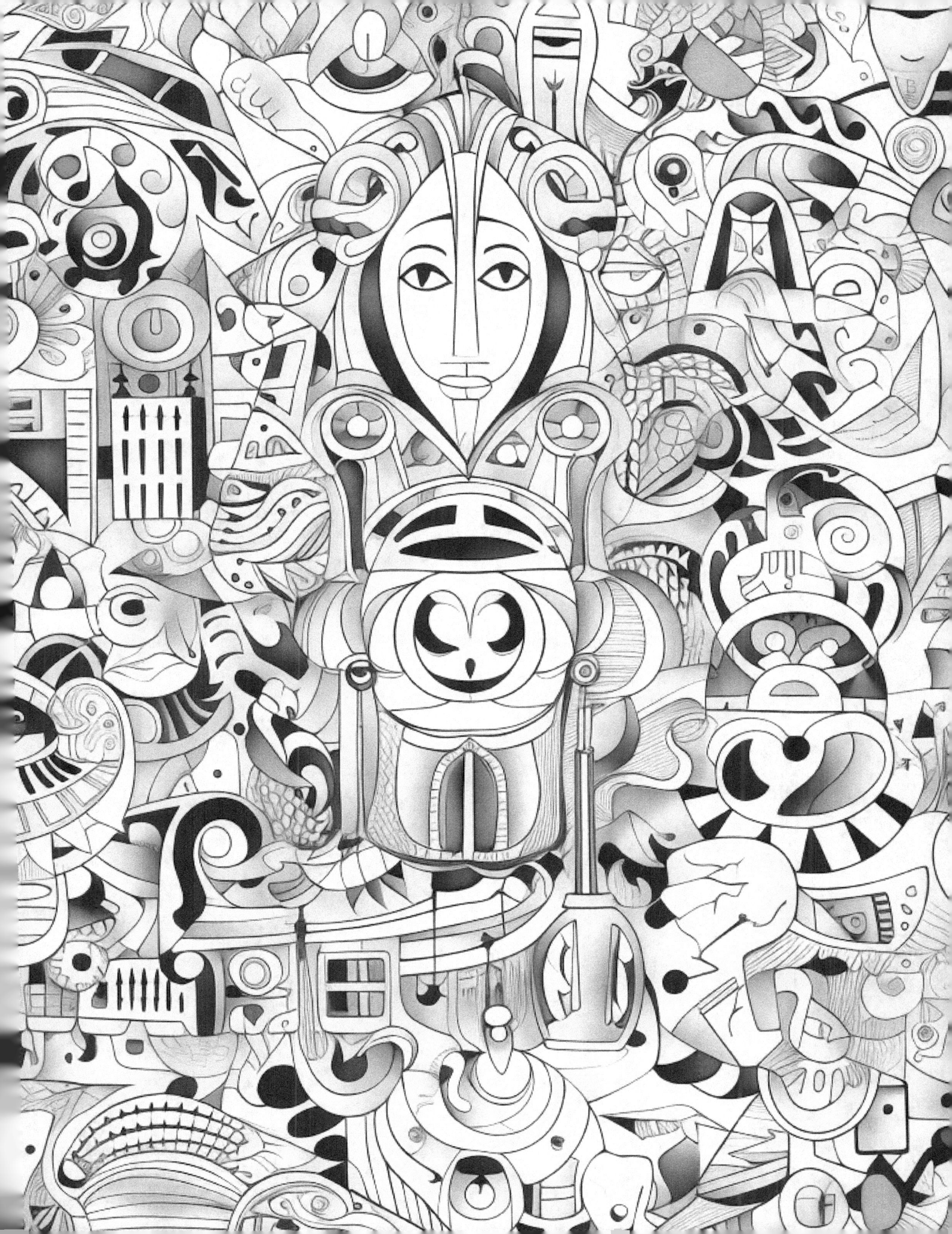

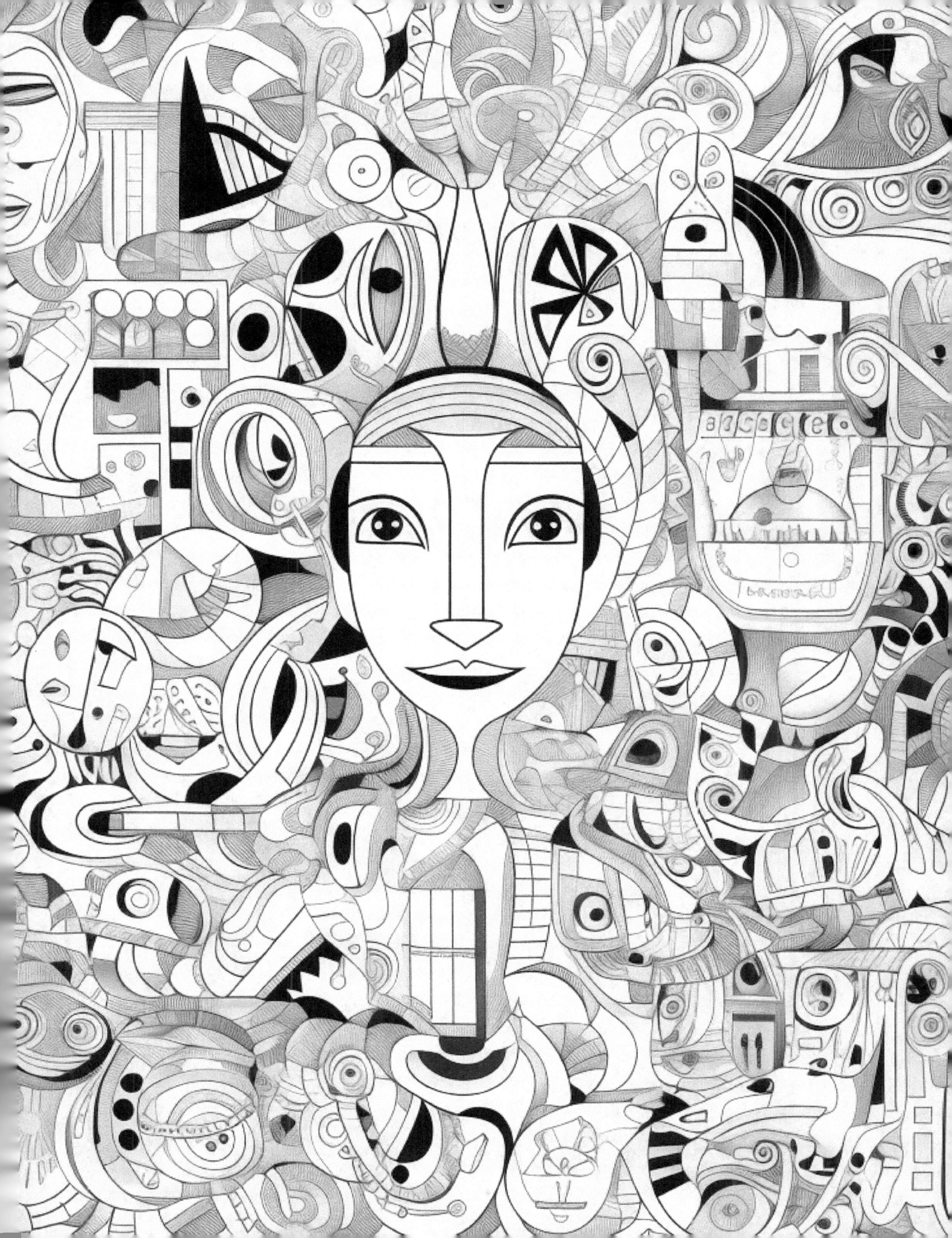

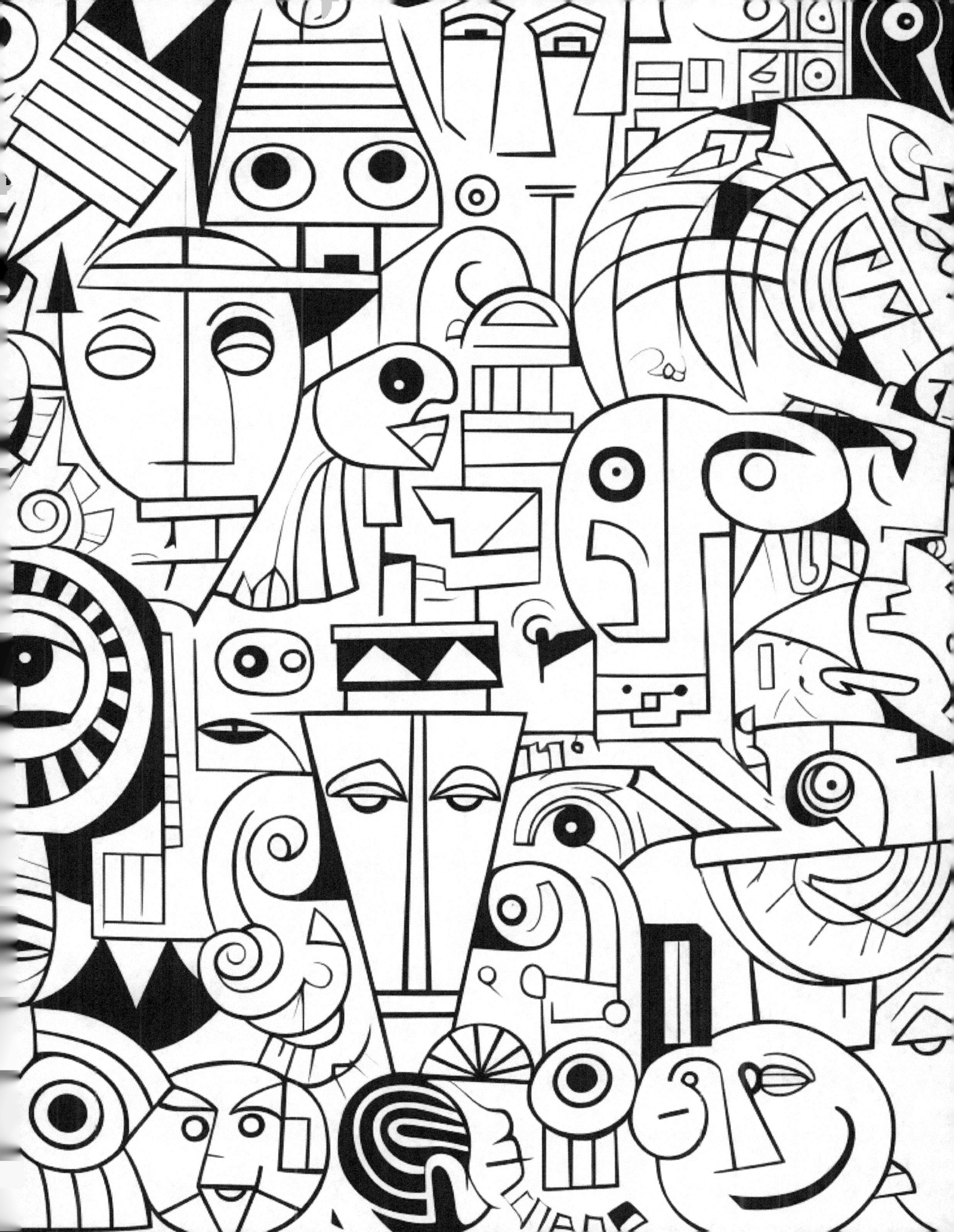

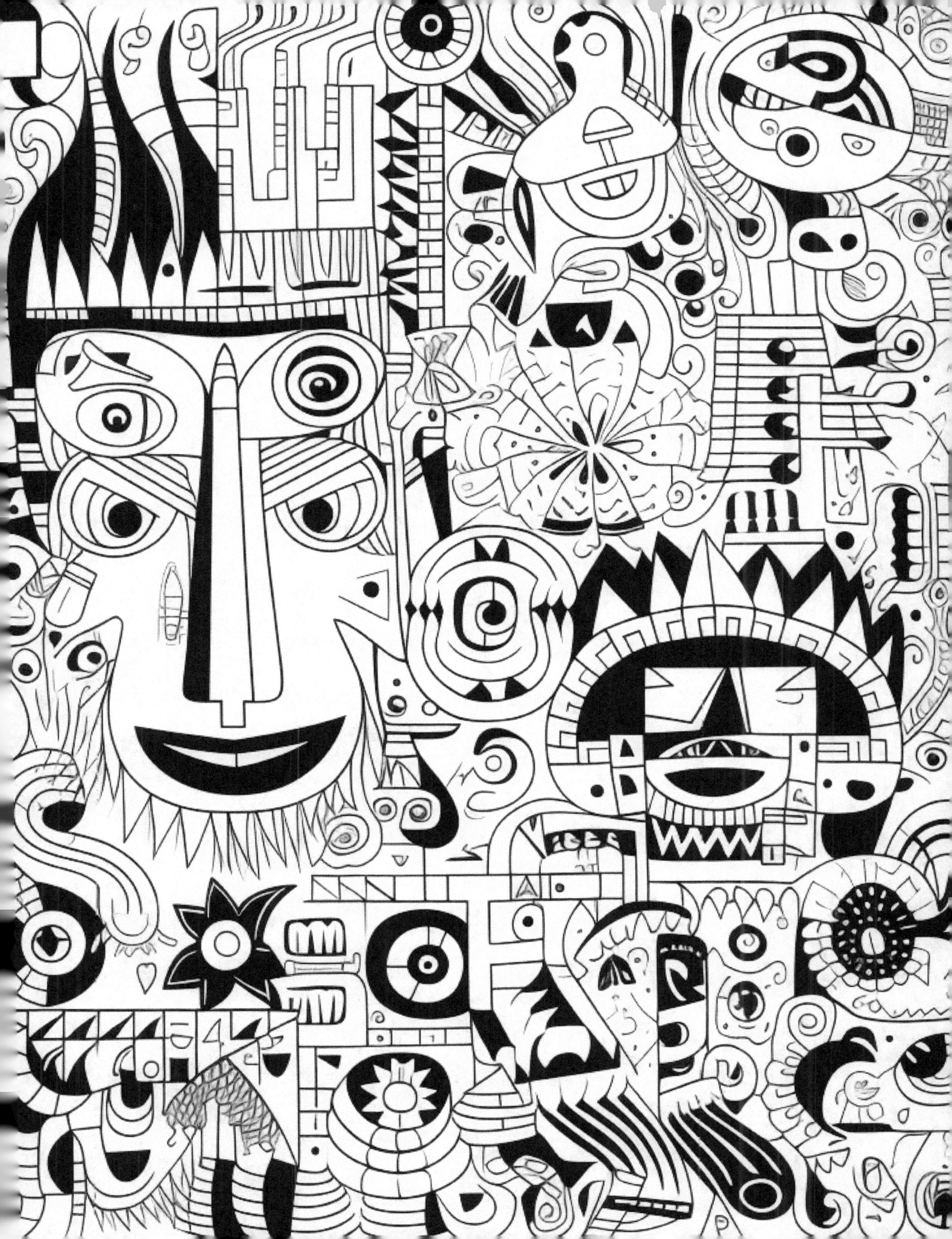

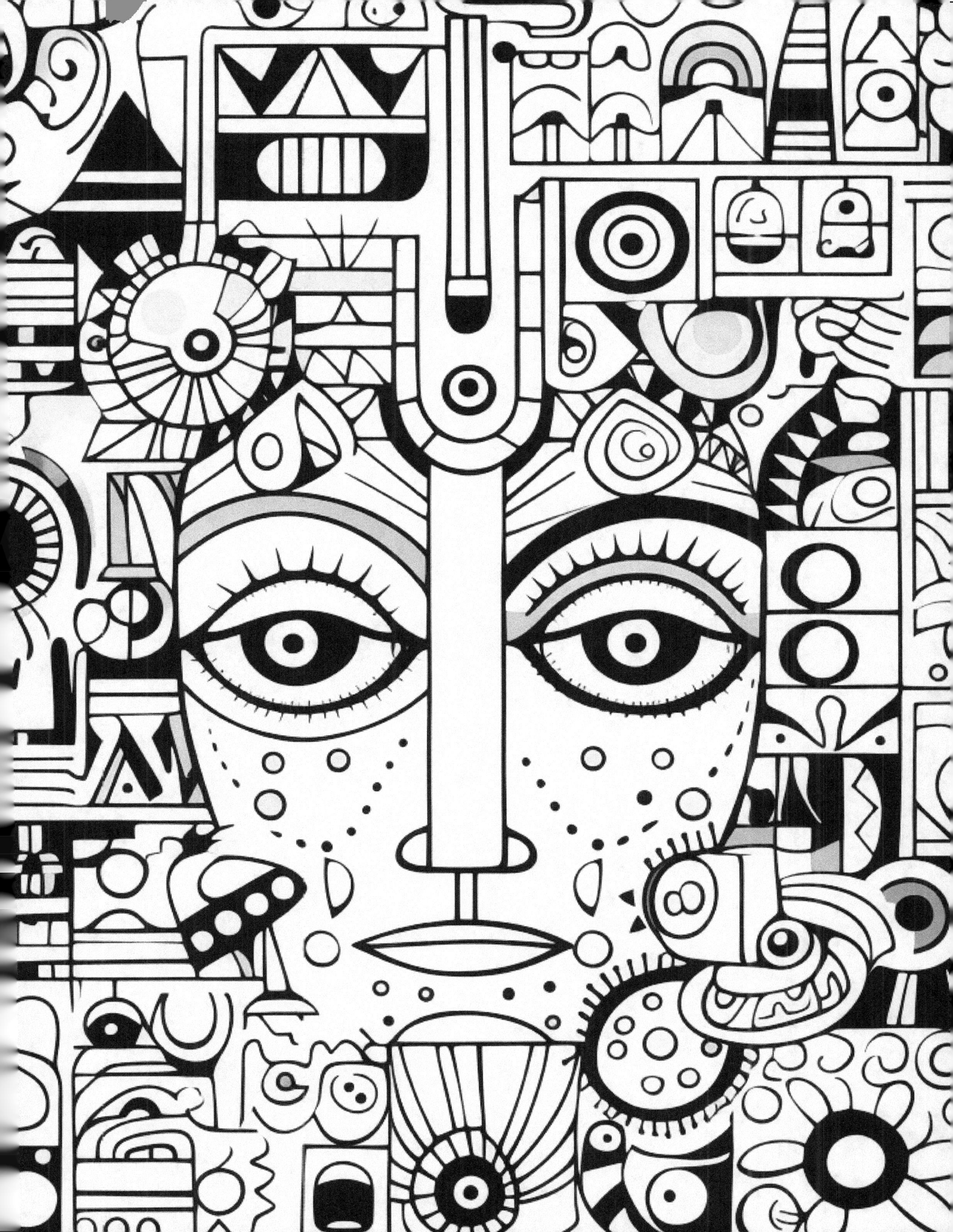

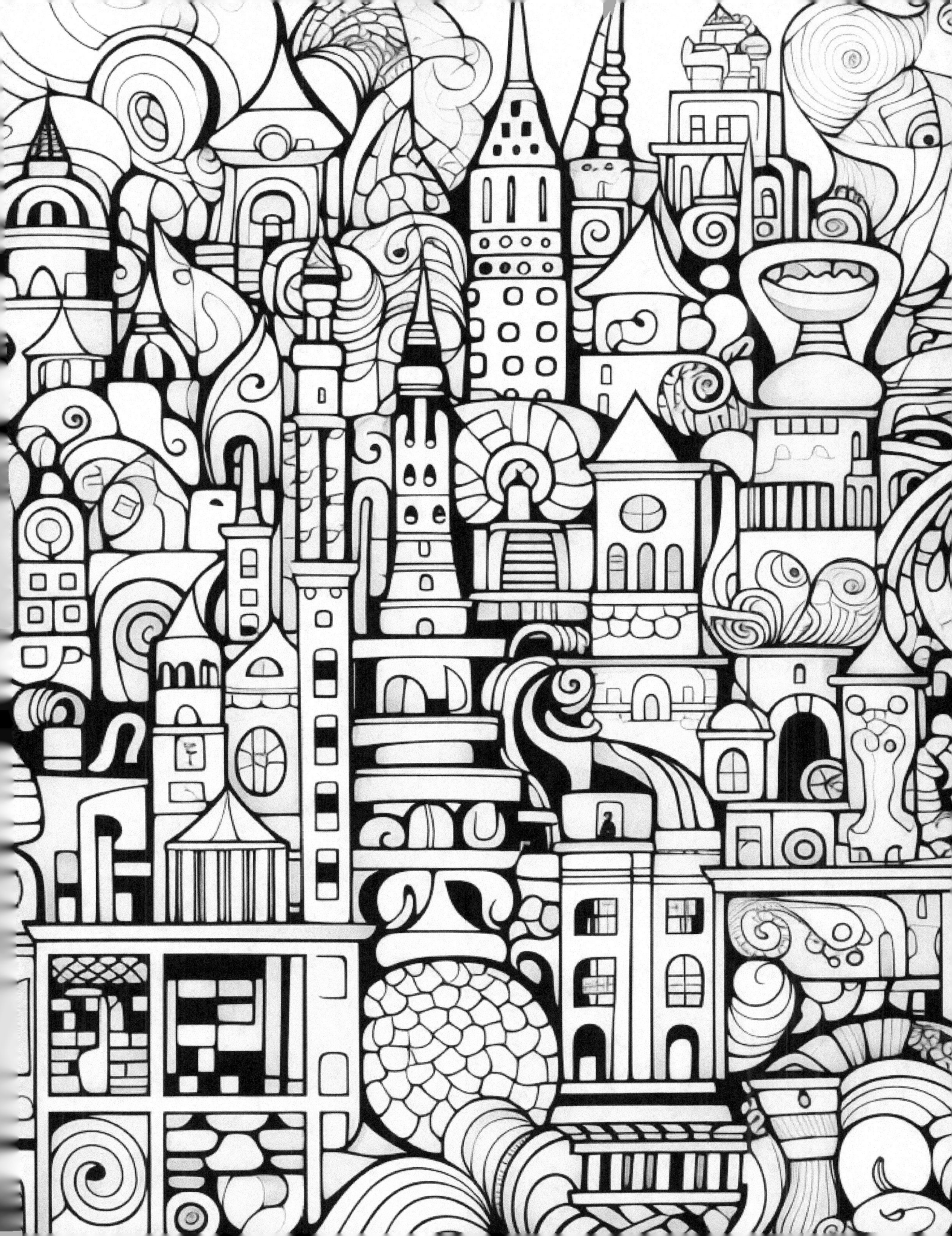

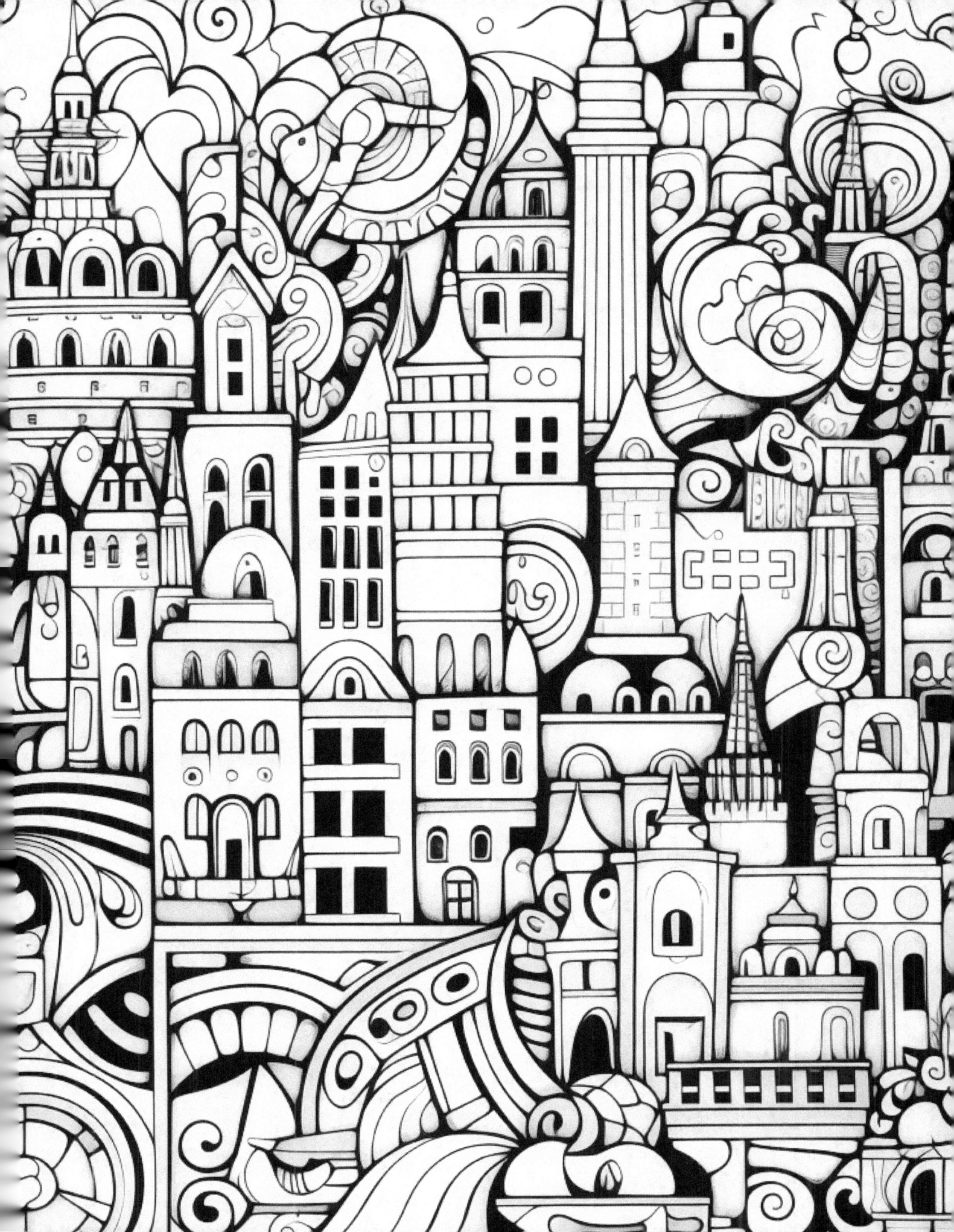

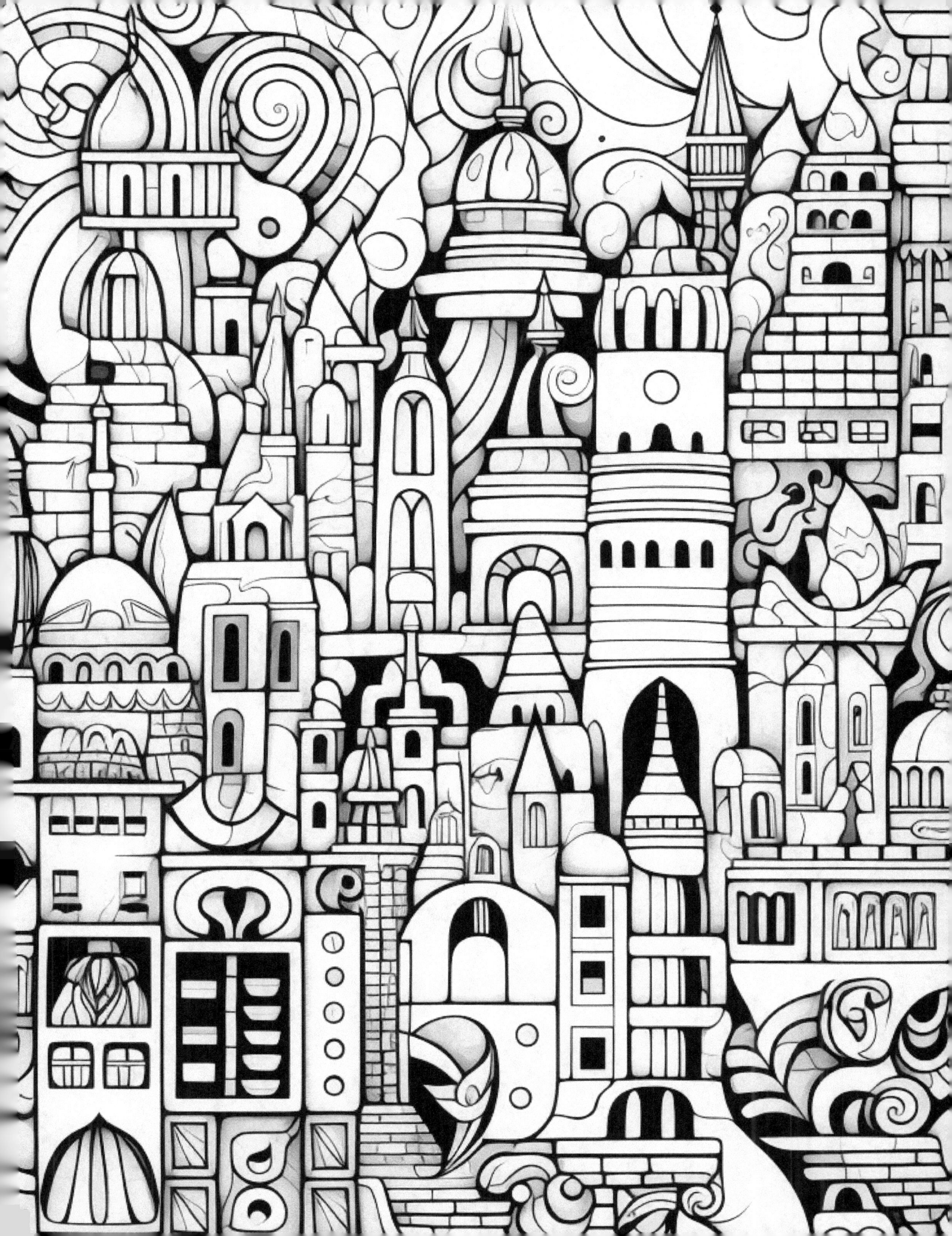

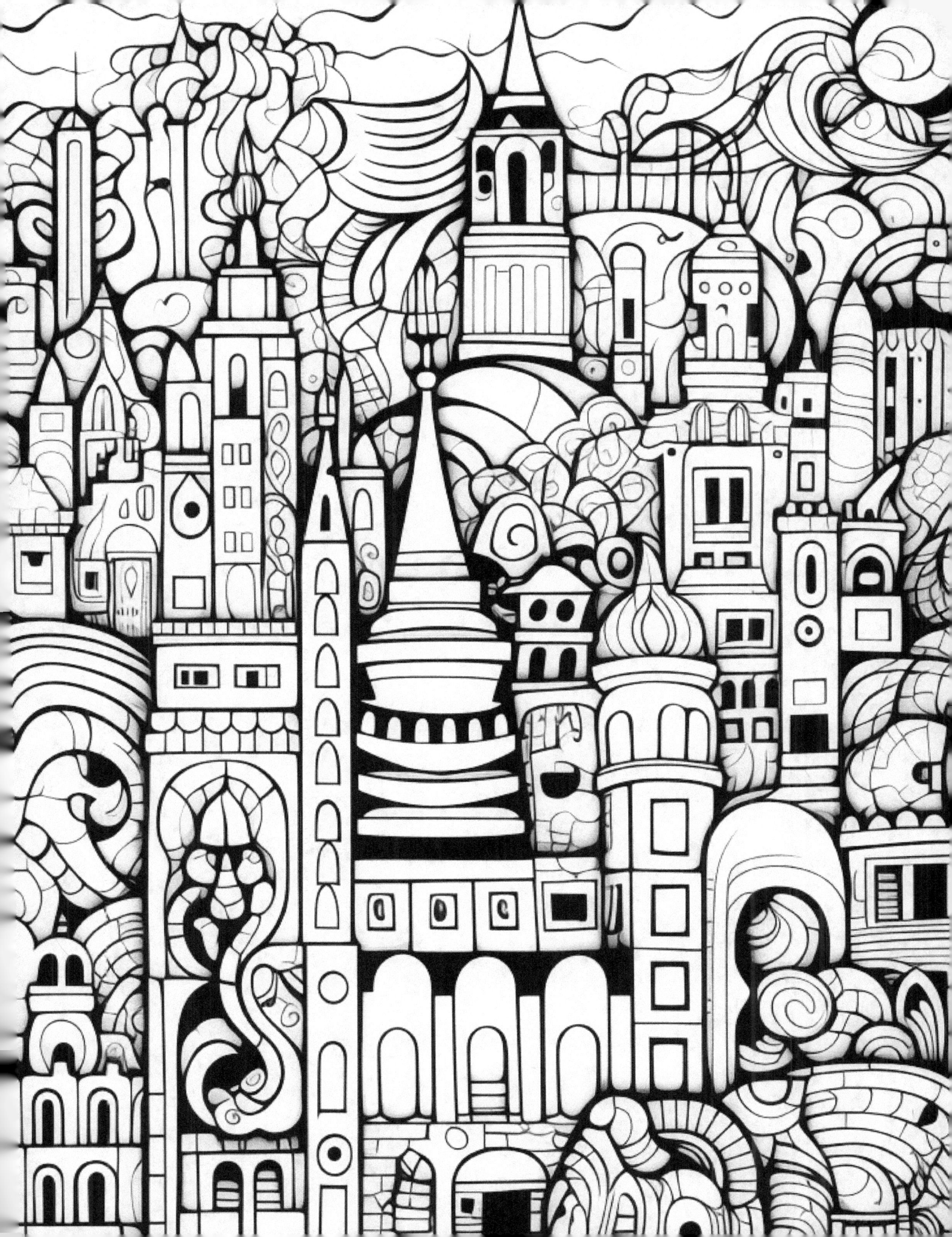

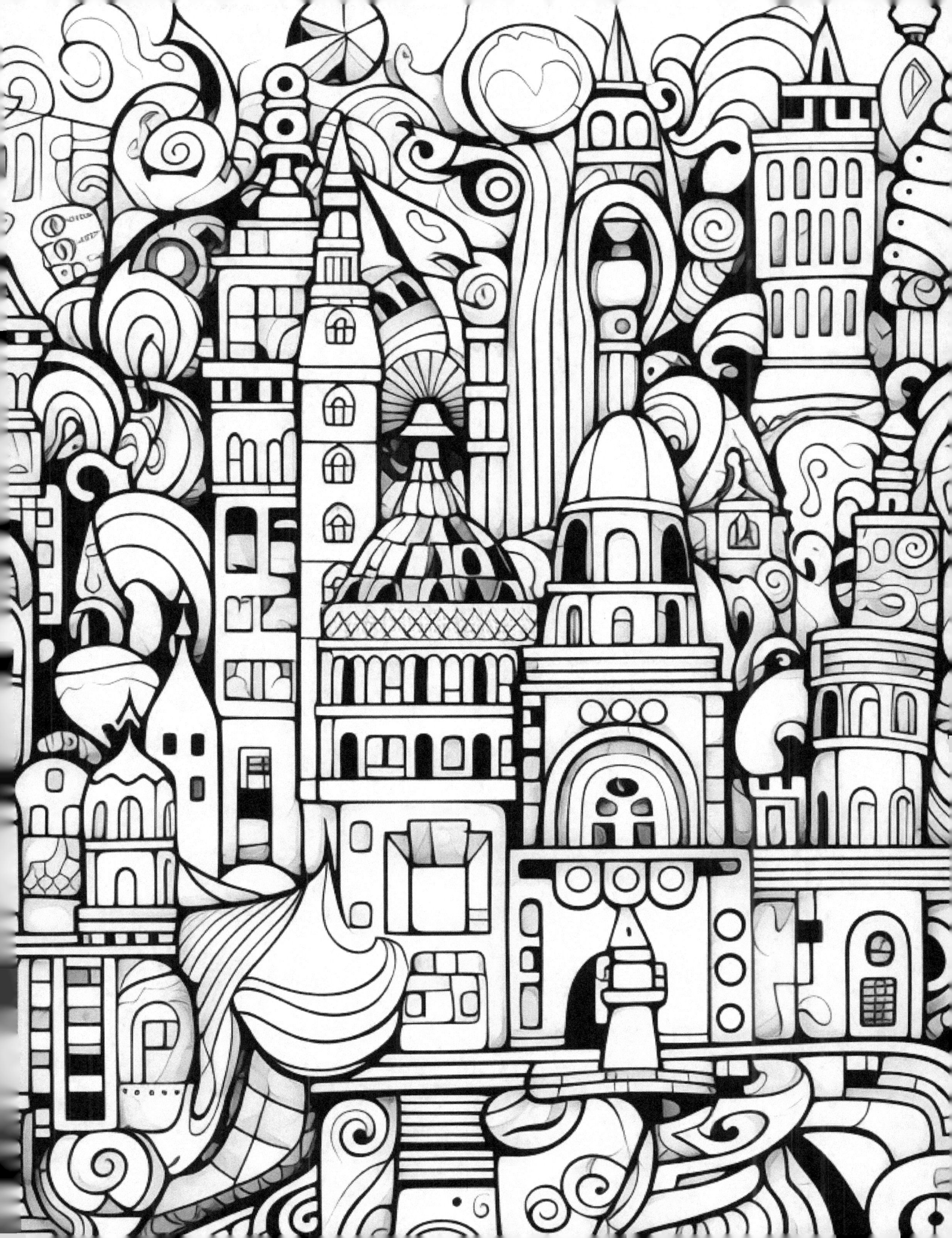

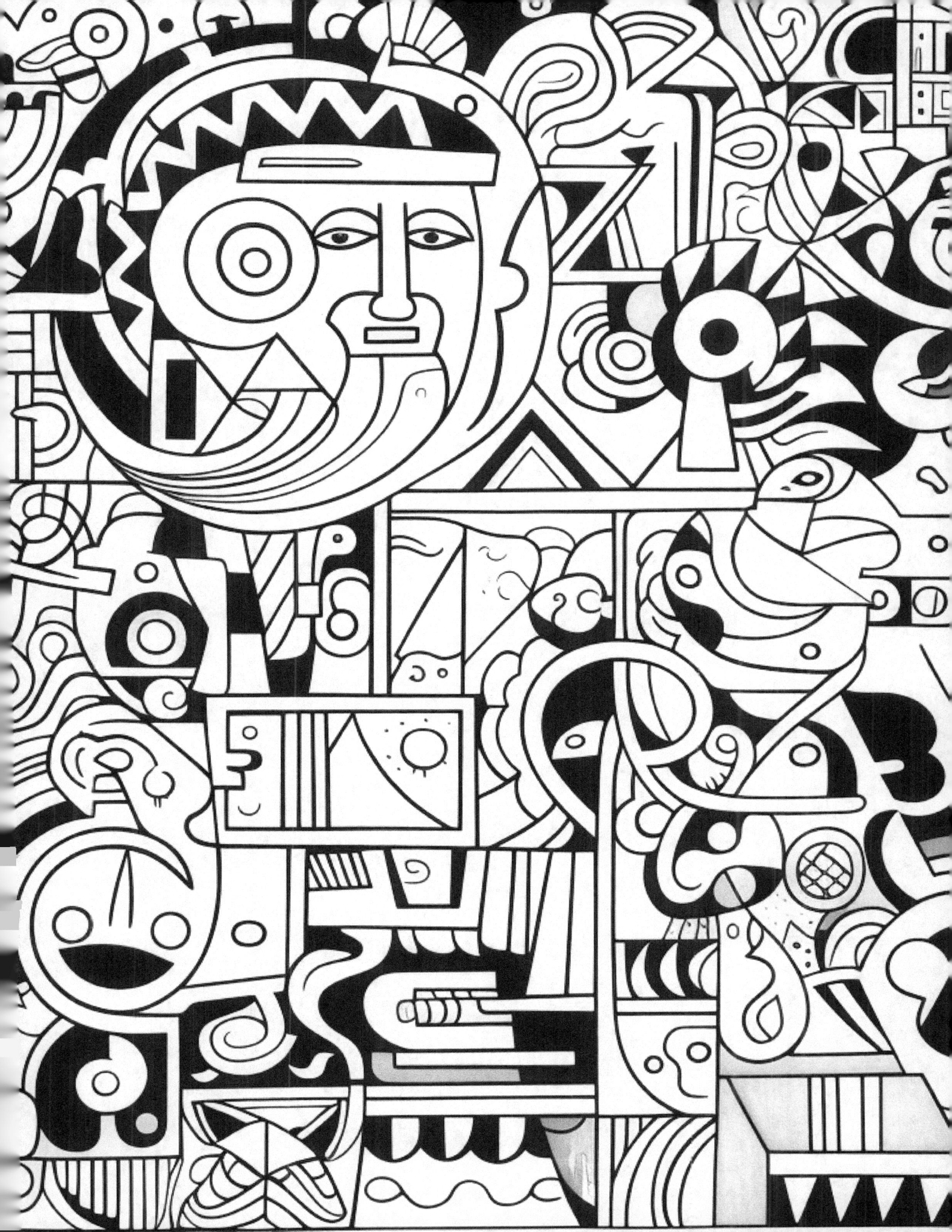

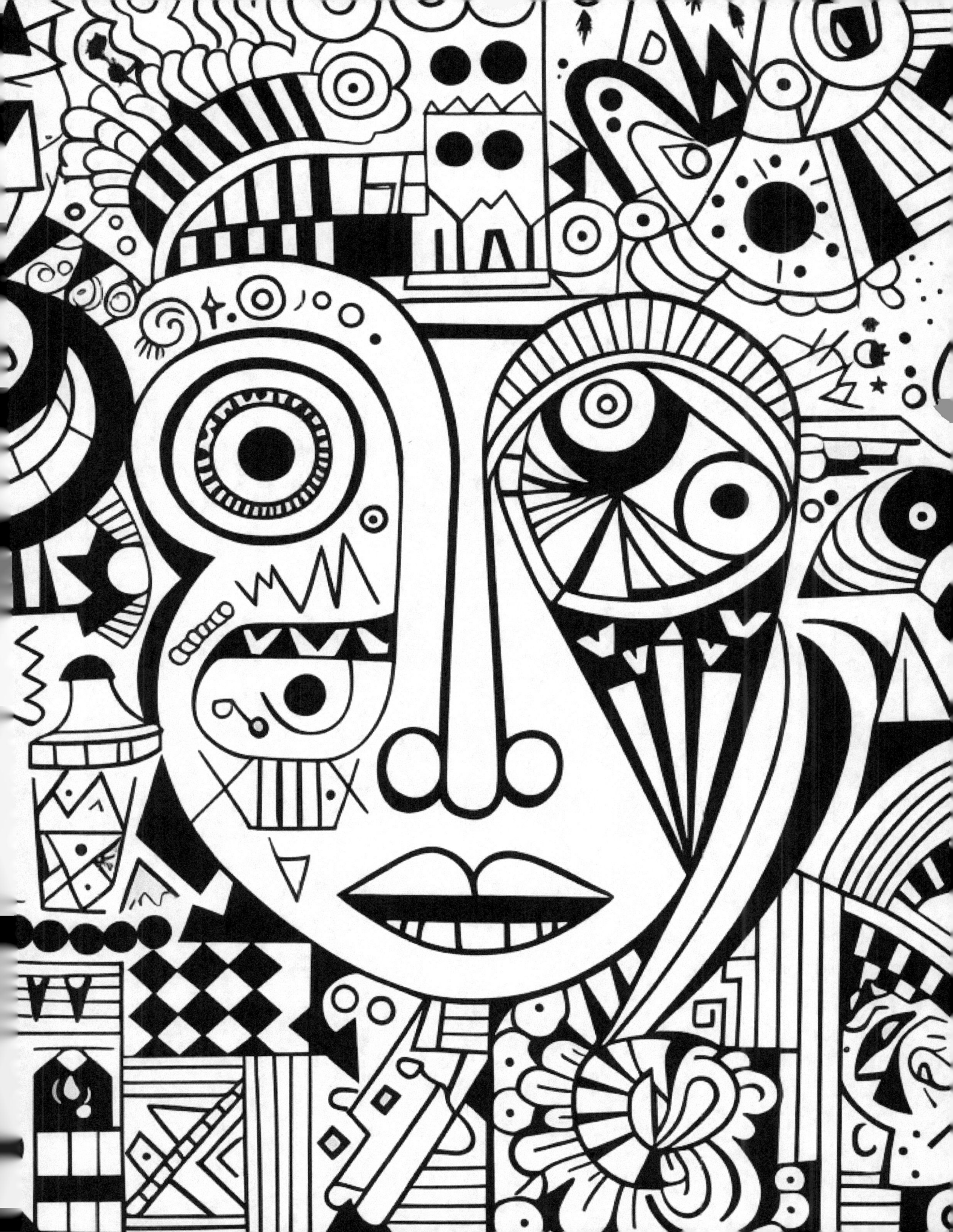

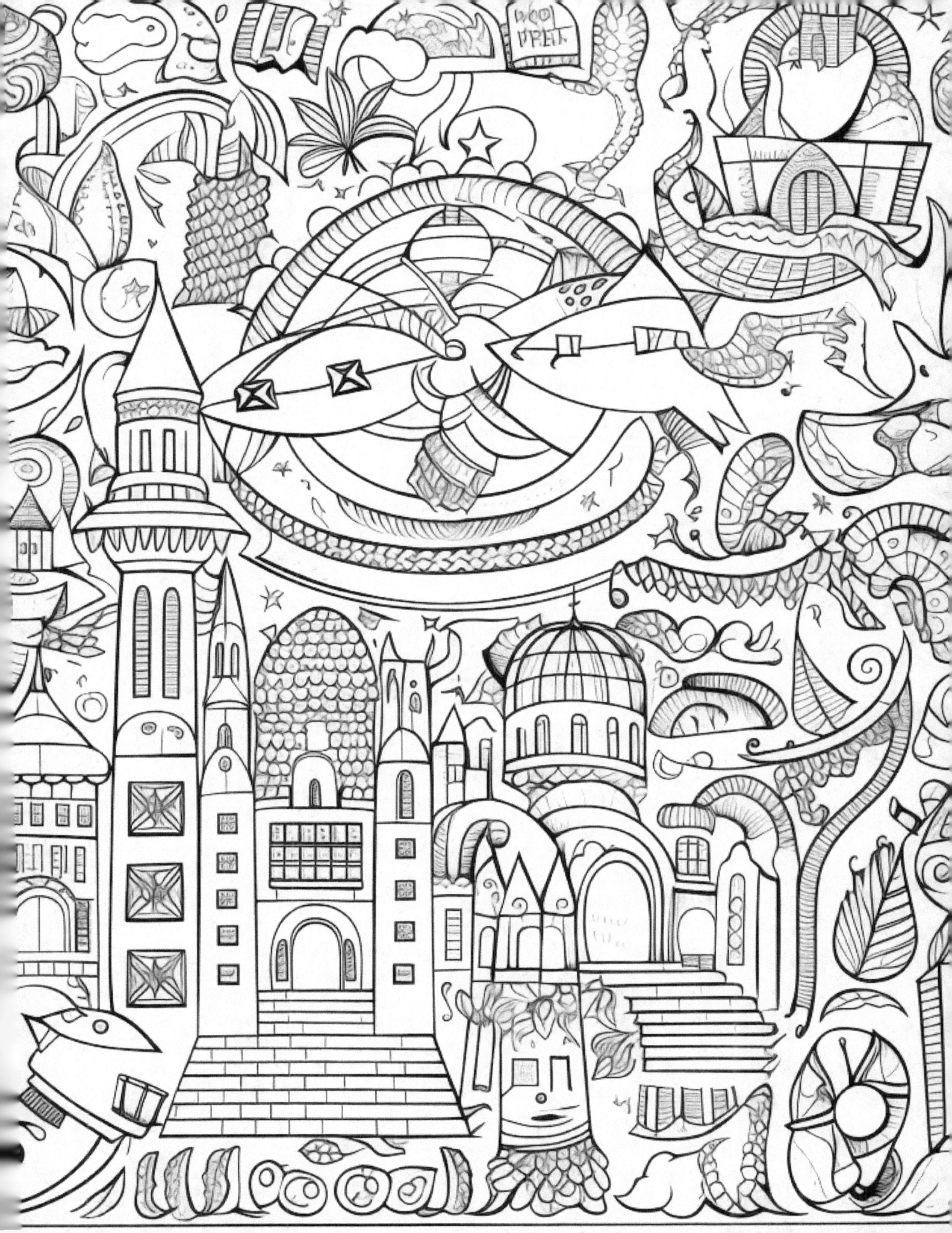

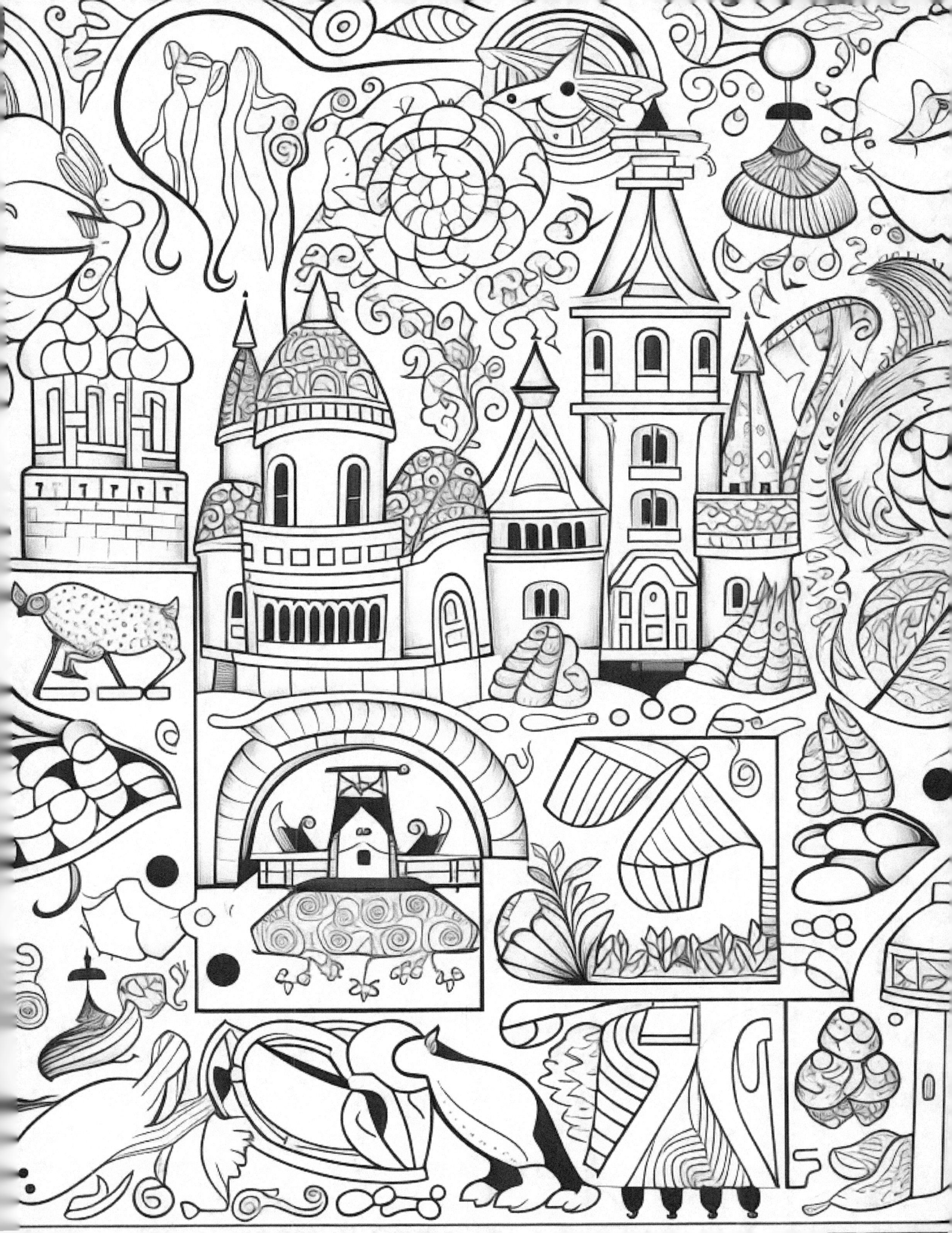

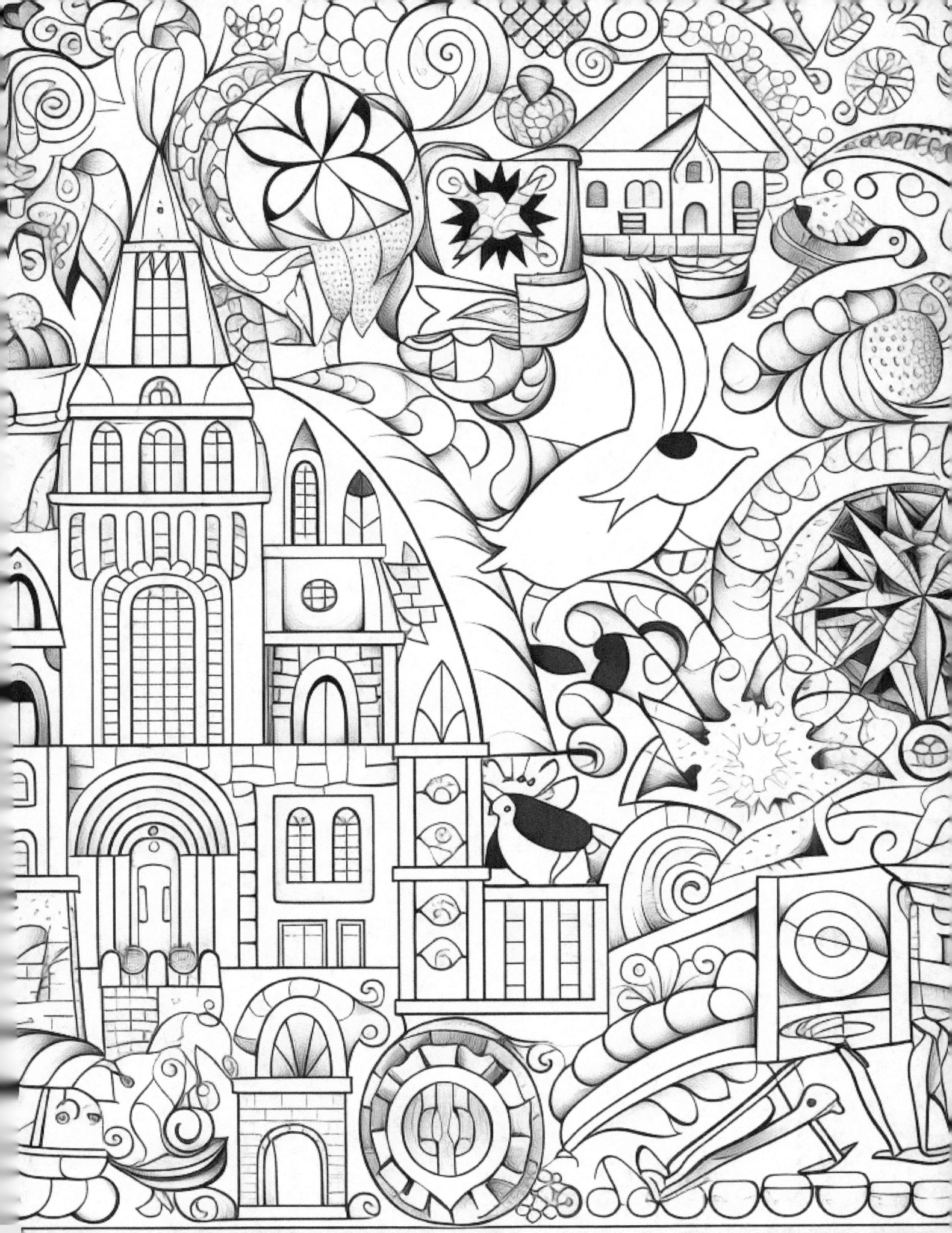

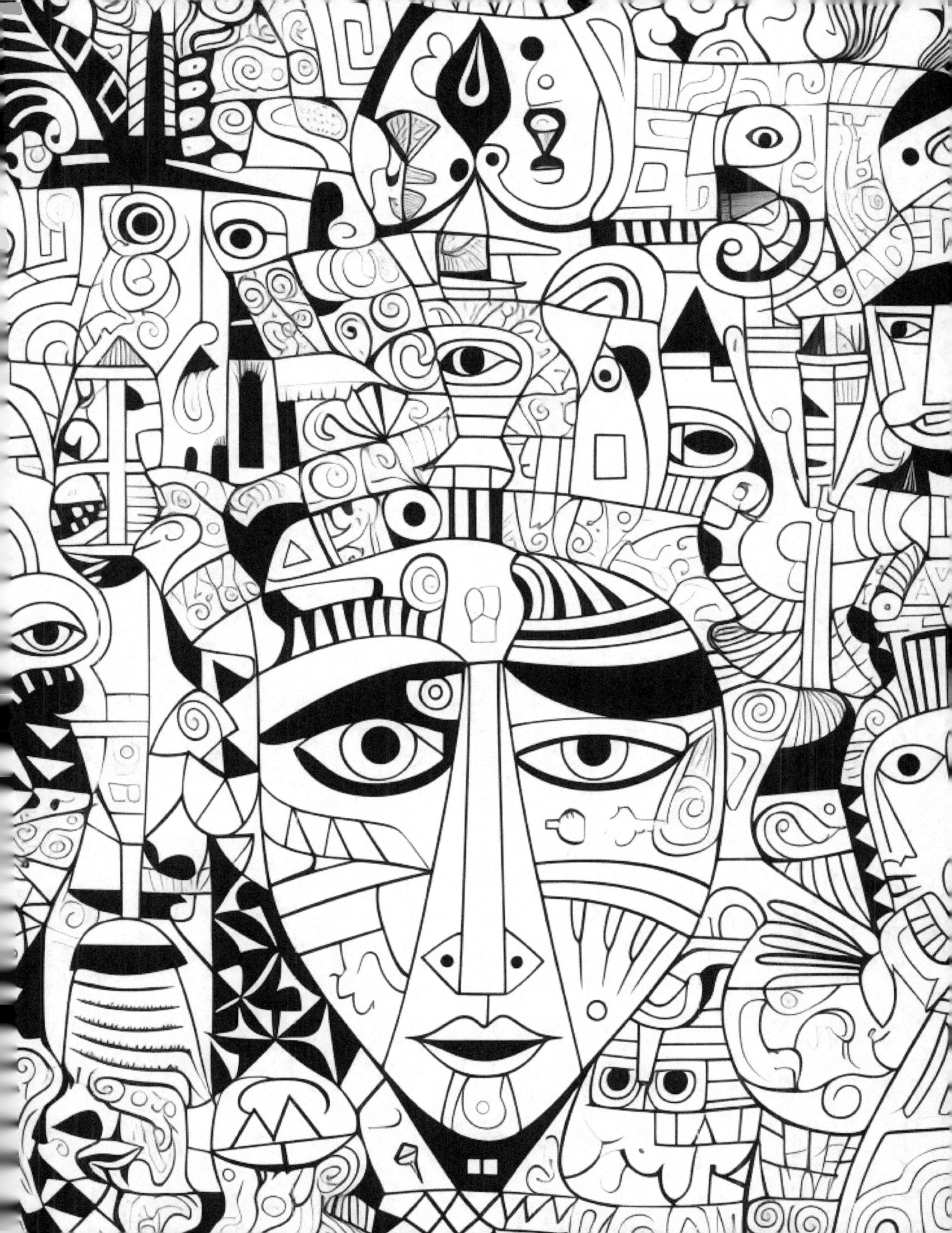

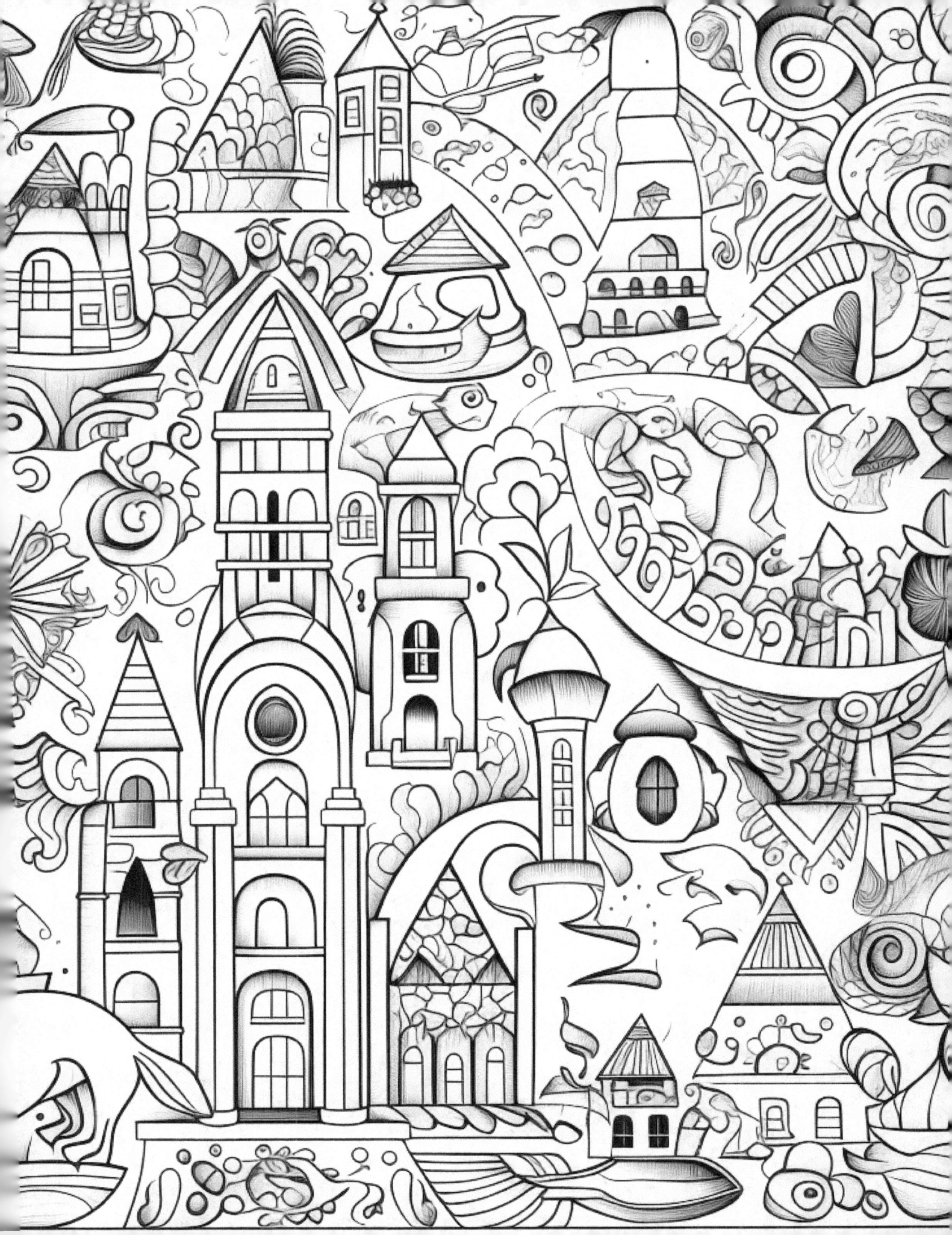

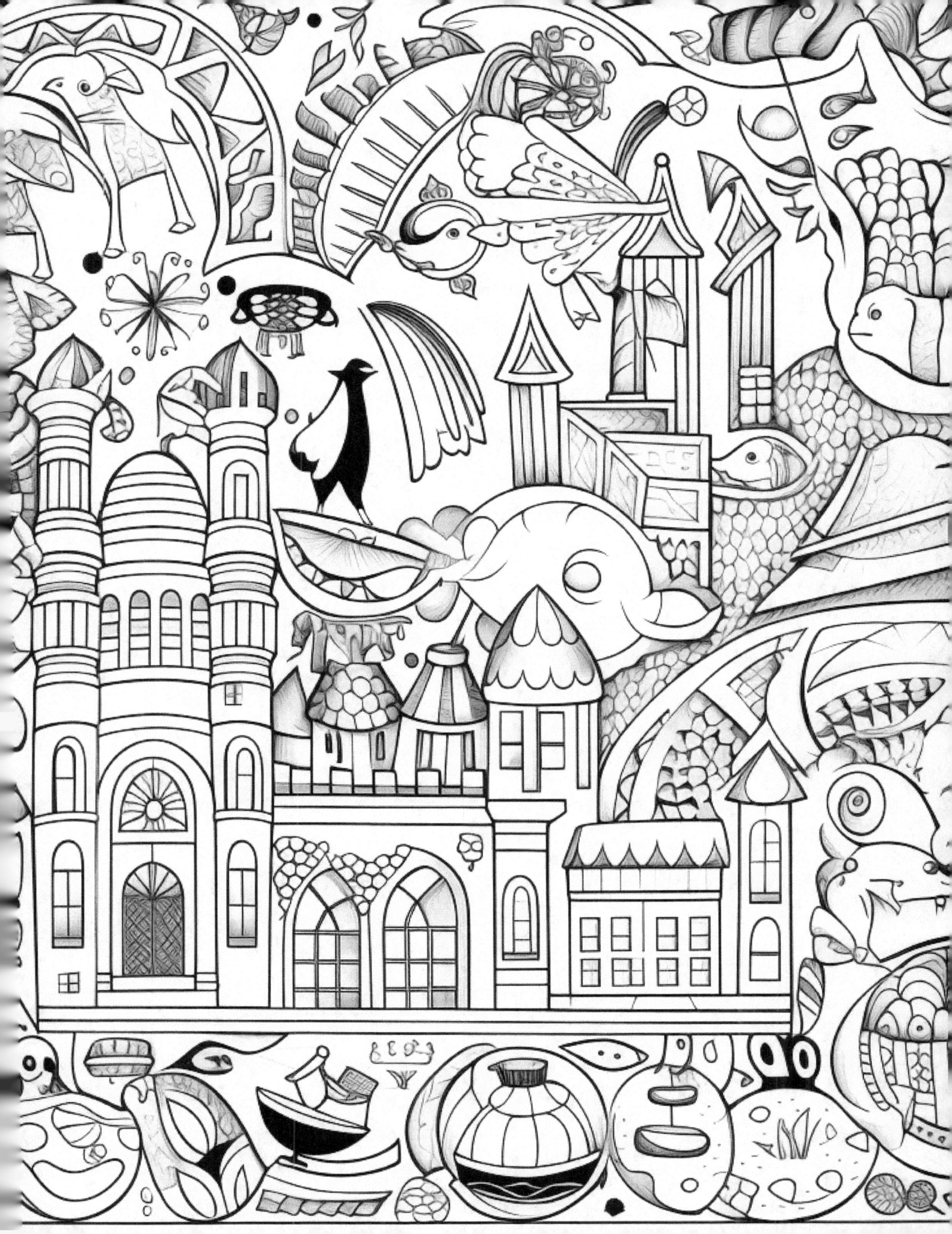

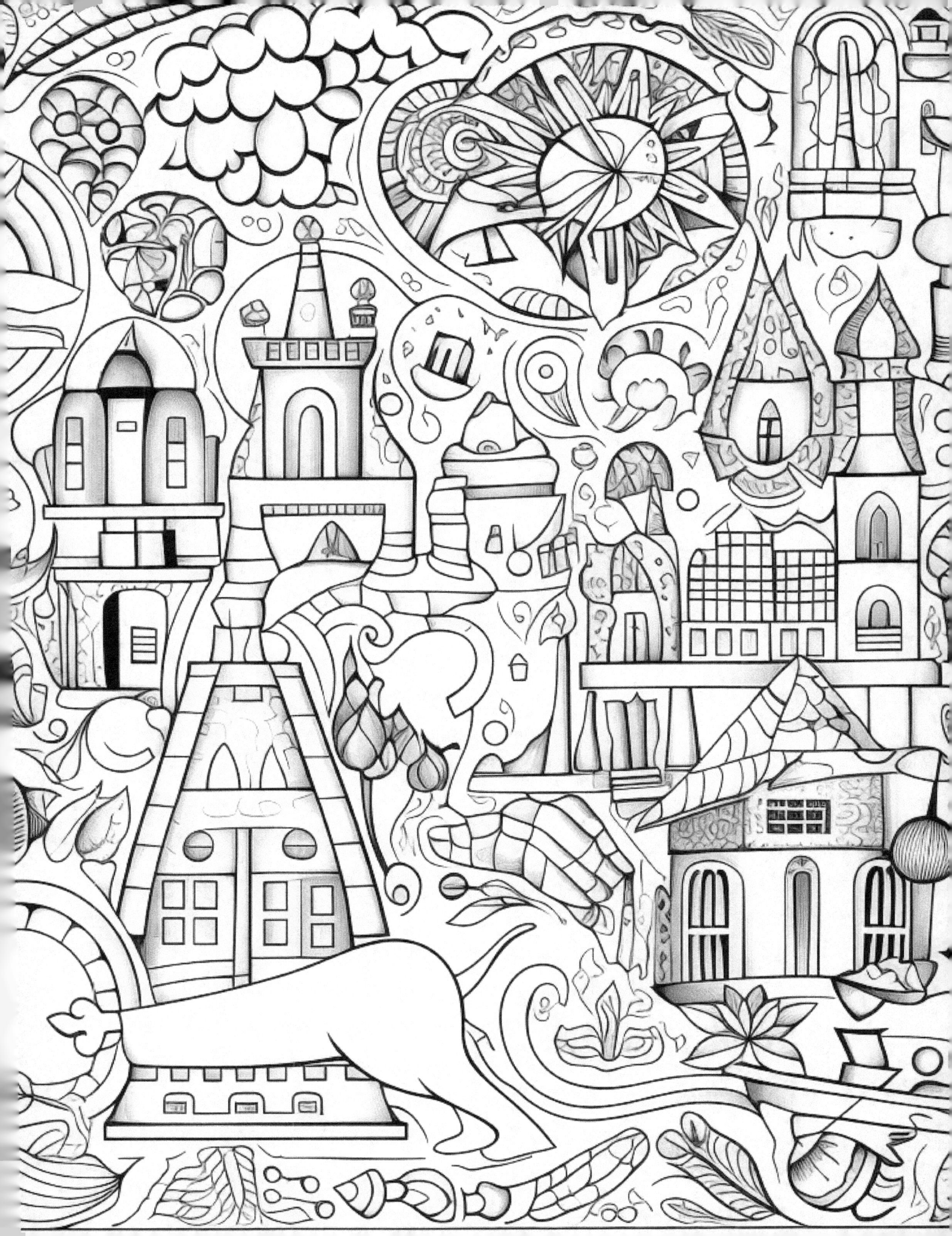

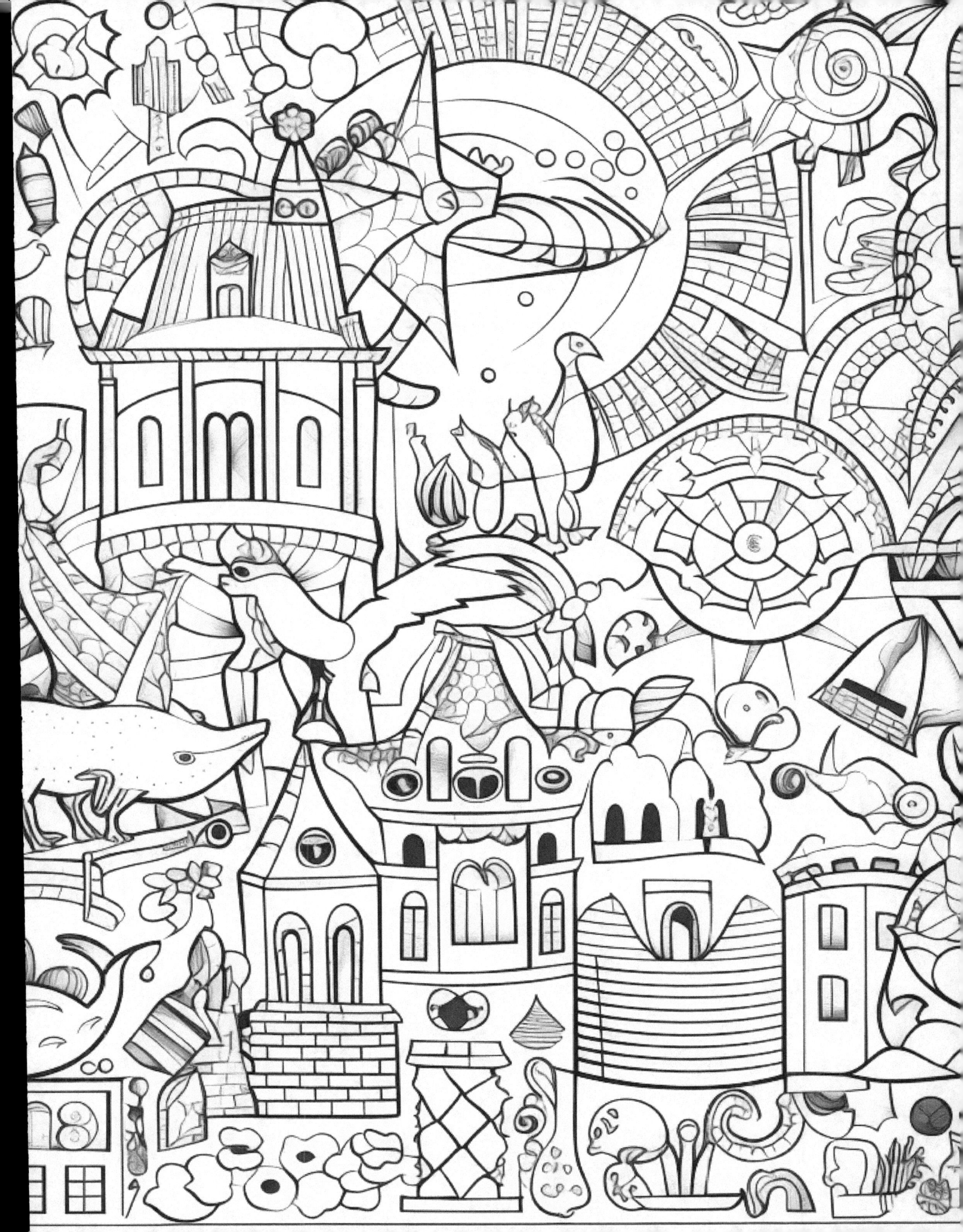

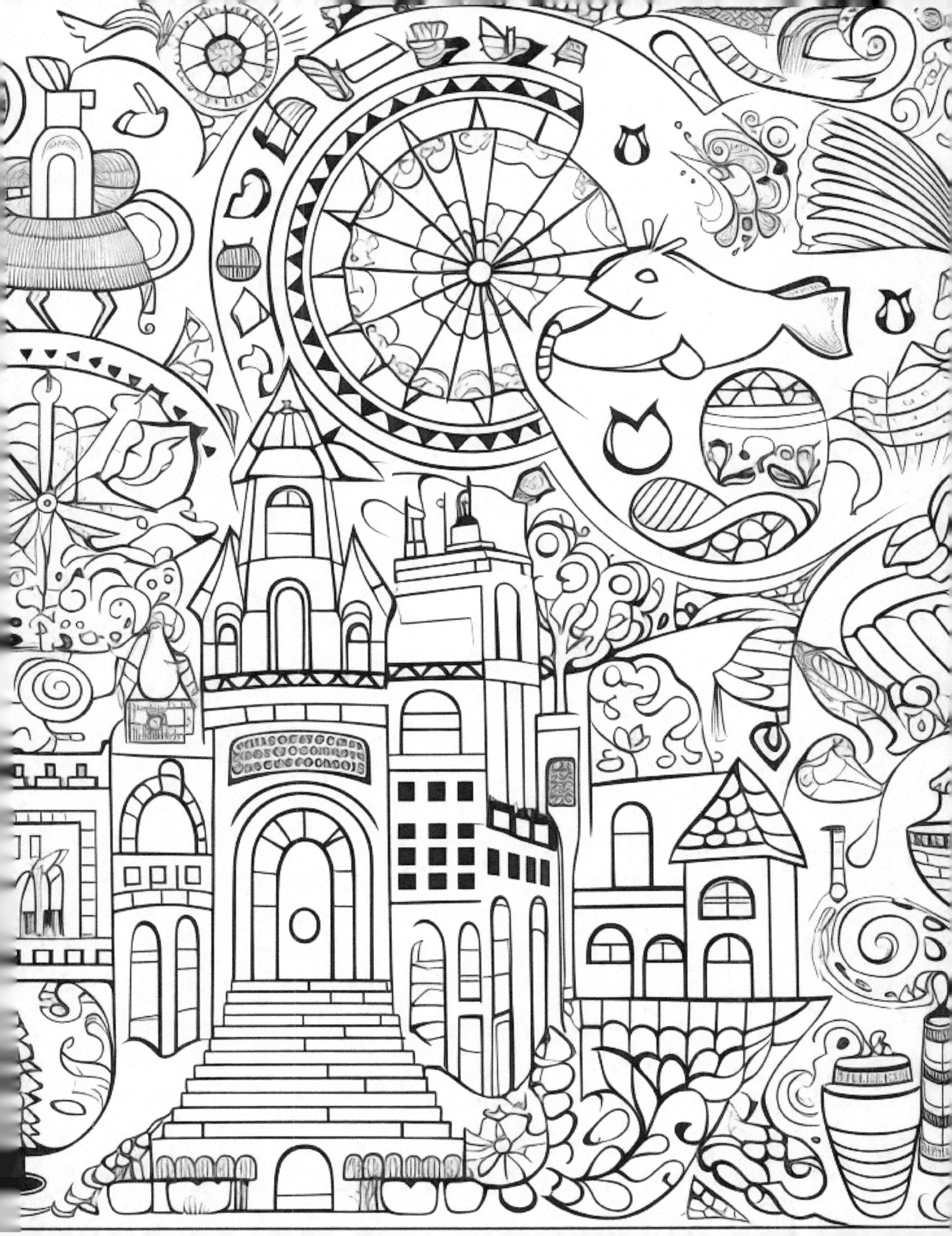

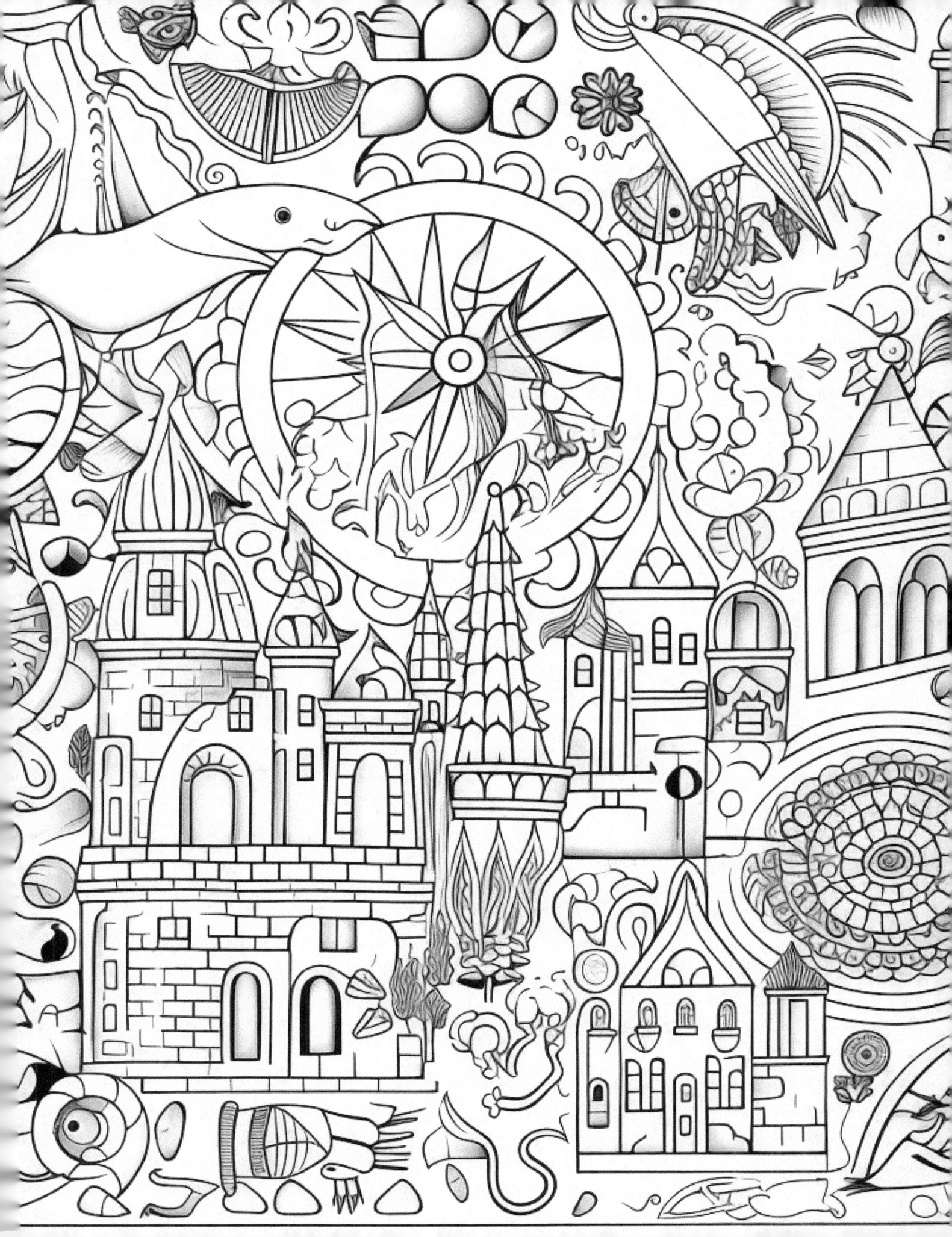

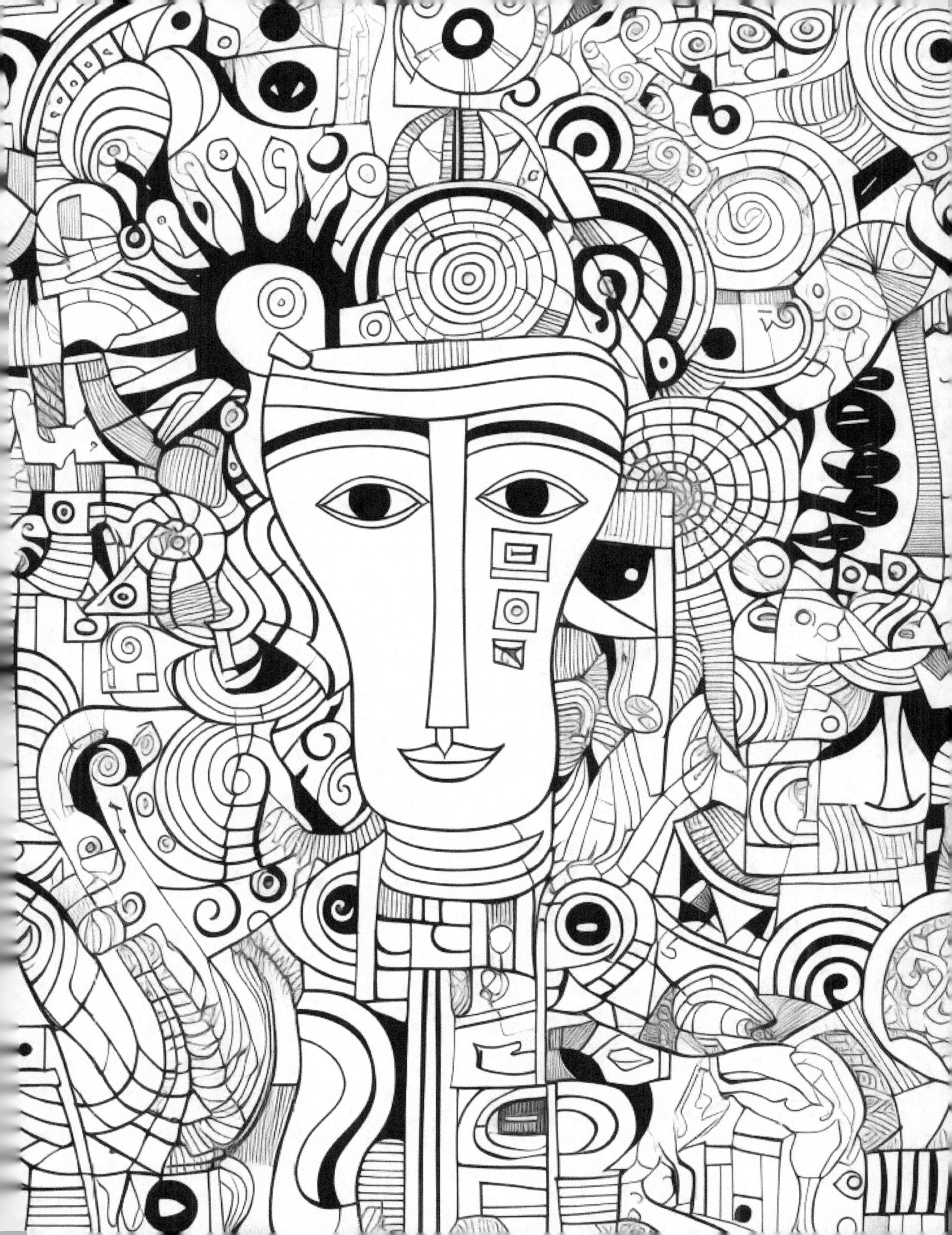

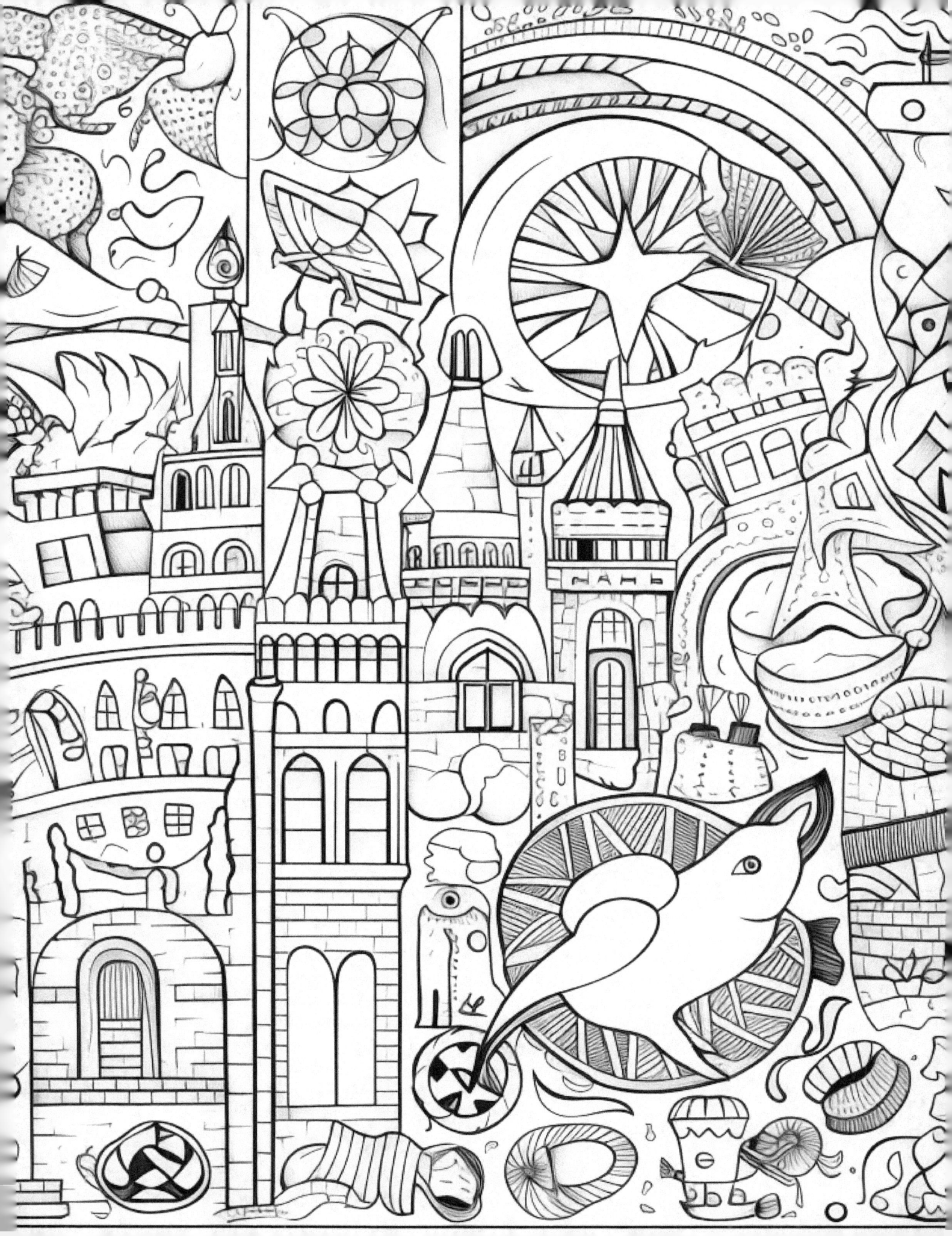

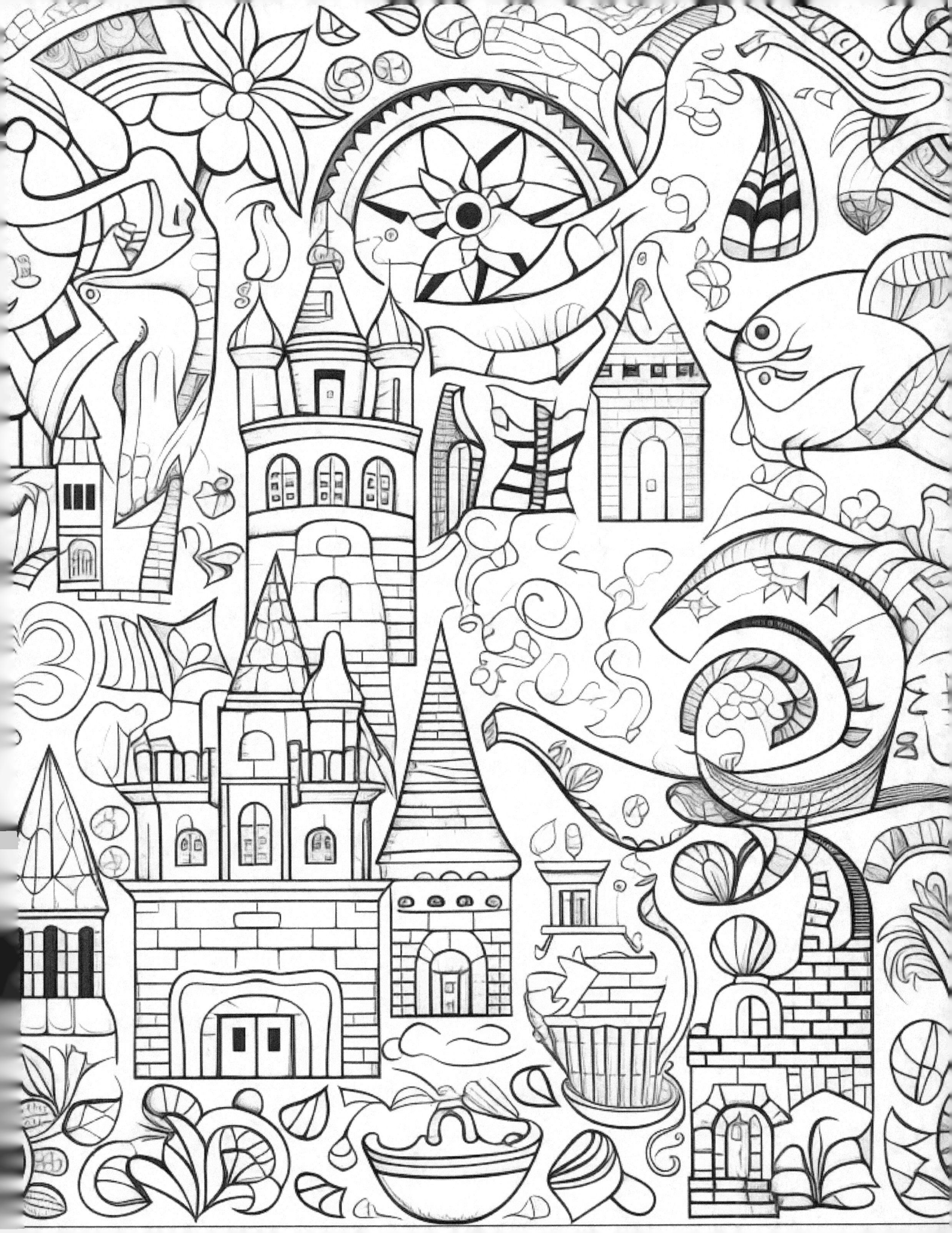

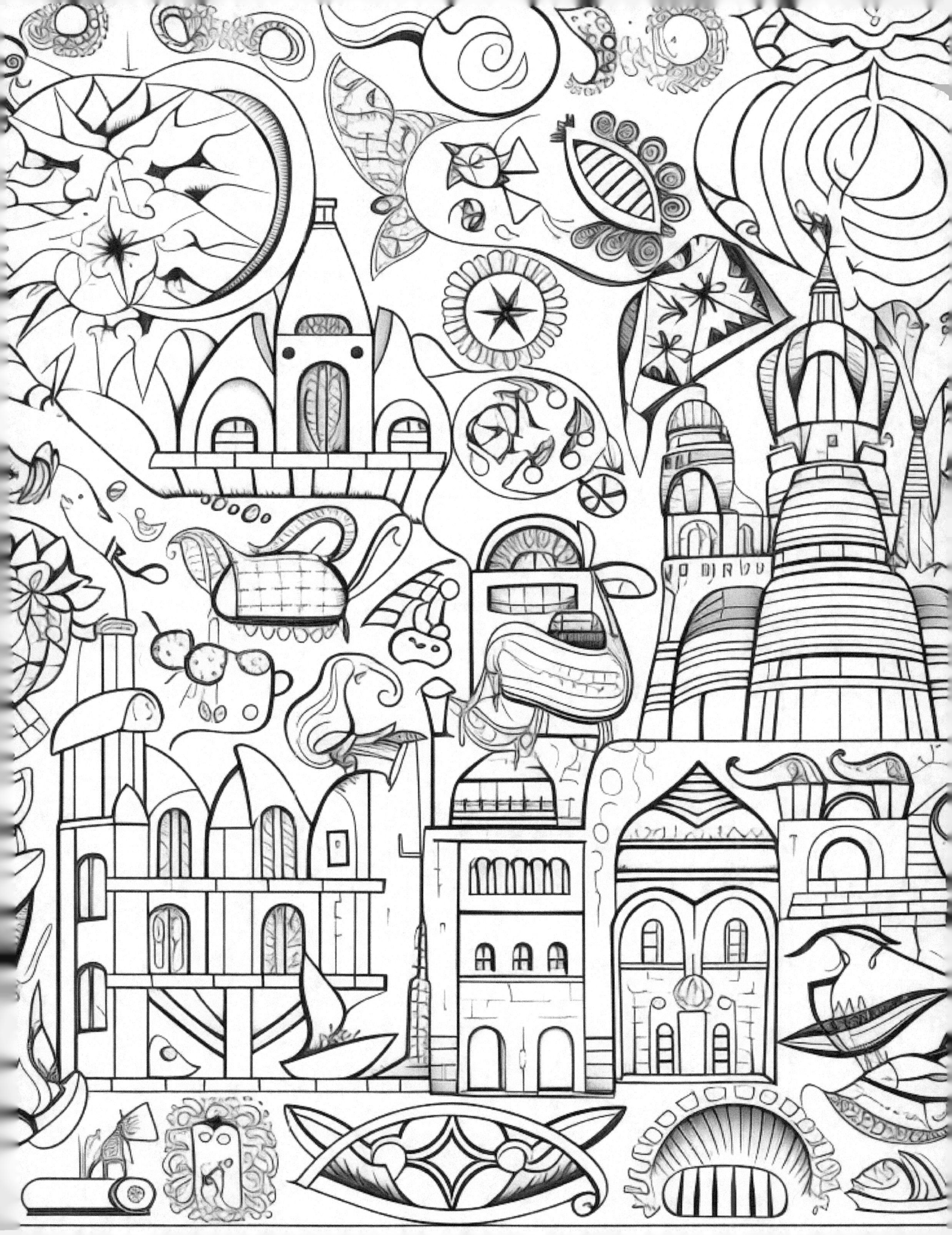

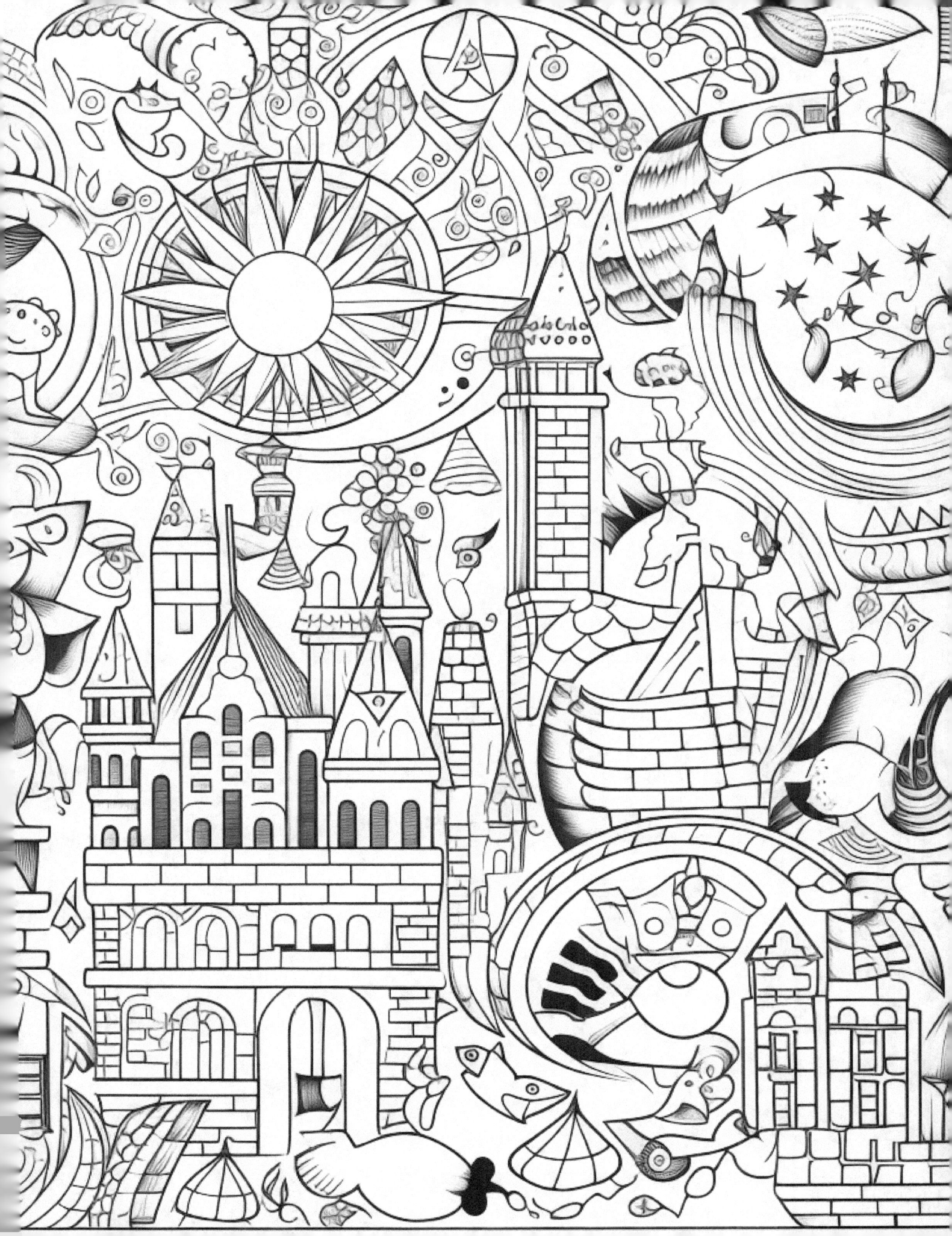

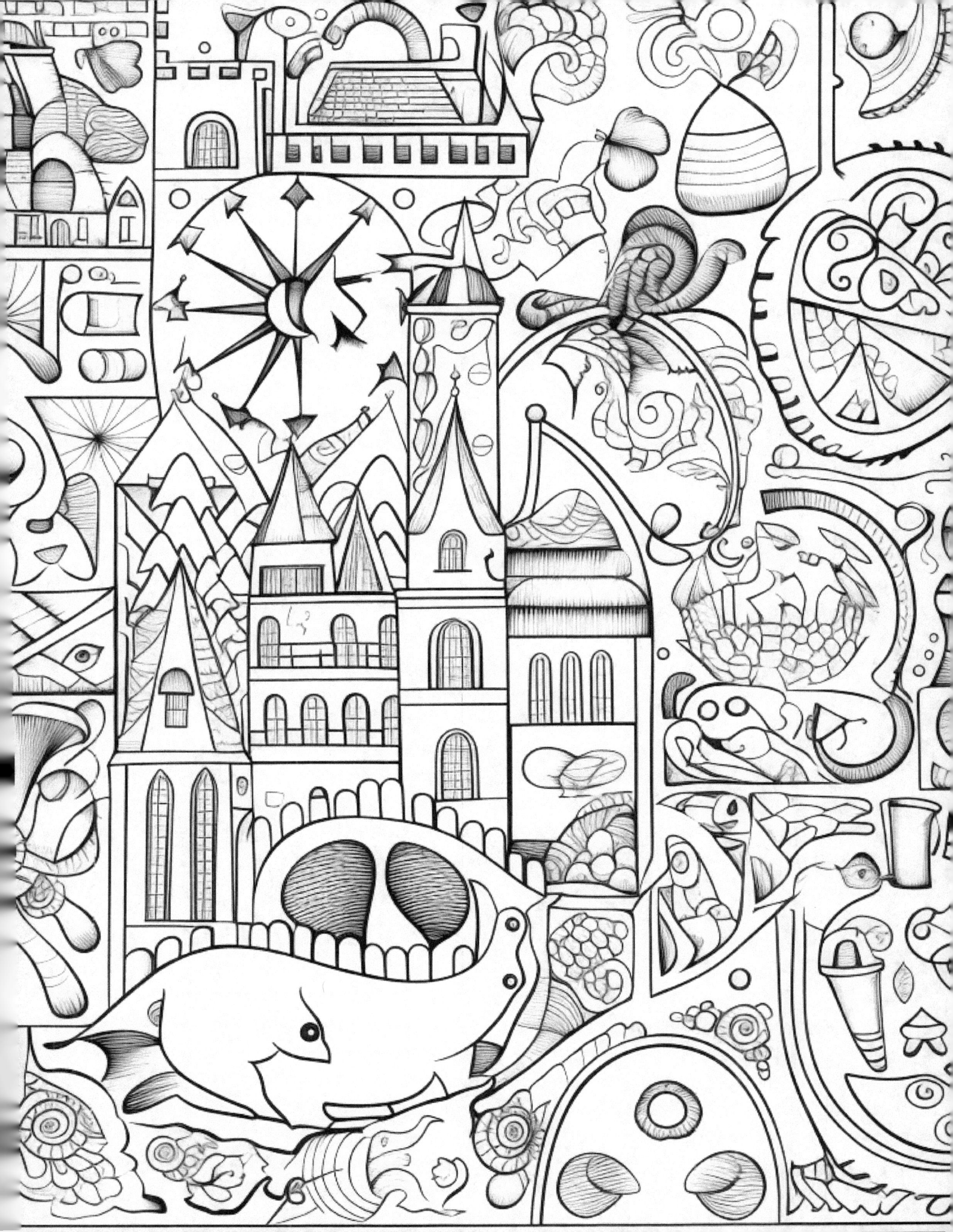